PREFACE

The study of algorithms is fundamental to the field of computer science and engineering, and it forms the backbone of software development, data processing, and problem-solving. The course MCS-211: Design and Analysis of Algorithms, offered by the Indira Gandhi National Open University (IGNOU), is pivotal for students pursuing a degree in computer science. The rigorous curriculum of this course requires students to not only understand the theoretical aspects of algorithms but also to apply this knowledge in solving complex computational problems. To assist students in their journey of mastering this subject, this book presents a comprehensive collection of previous years' unsolved papers of the MCS-211 course.The rationale behind compiling these unsolved papers is to provide students with a valuable resource that will enhance their understanding of the subject and prepare them effectively for examinations. These papers serve as an essential tool for self-assessment, allowing students to gauge their knowledge, identify areas that require further study, and practice solving problems within the time constraints typically imposed by examinations. Moreover, working through these papers helps students develop the analytical thinking and problem-solving skills necessary to excel in the field of algorithms.

This book is meticulously organized to cater to the needs of students at various levels of understanding. Each paper included in this compilation is carefully selected from different years to represent a broad spectrum of topics covered in the MCS-211 syllabus. The problems range from basic algorithmic challenges to more complex scenarios that test a student's ability to design efficient and effective algorithms. By attempting these unsolved papers, students will not only reinforce their theoretical knowledge but also gain hands-on experience in tackling real-world algorithmic problems.In addition to serving as an academic resource, this book is also intended to instill confidence in students as they prepare for their examinations. The exposure to a variety of problems will familiarize students with the types of questions that are likely to appear in exams, enabling them to approach their studies with a strategic mindset. This book encourages a deeper exploration of the subject, prompting students to engage with the material beyond the standard textbook content and to think critically about the design and analysis of algorithms.

We would like to express our gratitude to the students and educators who have contributed to the development of this book. Their insights and feedback have been invaluable in ensuring that this compilation meets the highest standards of academic excellence. As you embark on your journey through the world of algorithms, we hope that this book will be a reliable companion in your studies, helping you to unlock the full potential of your capabilities in the field of computer science.

Table of Contents

Master In Computer Application (MCA)
Chapter 1: Term-End Examination, December, 2022
MCS-231: Mobile Computing

Time: 3 Hours
Maximum Marks: 100
Note: Question No. 1 is compulsory and carries 40 marks. Attempt any three questions from the rest.

1. (a) What is Frequency Division Multiplexing (FDM)? What are its advantages, disadvantages and applications? 10

(b) What is GPRS? Explain its features. Also, list the services offered by it. 10

(c) What is LTE? Explain its features. 10

(d) Write a short note on the Adhoc Networks. 10

2. (a) What is a cellular network? Explain its various components. 10

(b) Explain mobile computing architecture with the help of a diagram. 10

3. (a) List any five applications of mobile computing. 10

(b) Explain J2EE architecture. 10

4. (a) Explain the functions of a mobile operating system. 10

(b) Explain the features of an integrated development platform for mobile apps. 10

5. (a) Explain the features of iOS. 10

(b) Explain the features of XML. 10

Master In Computer Application (MCA)
Chapter 2: Term-End Examination, June, 2023
MCS-231: Mobile Computing

Time: 3 Hours
Maximum Marks: 100
Note: Question No. 1 is compulsory and carries 40 marks. Attempt any three questions from the rest.

1. (a) What is Time Division Multiplexing (TDM)? What are the advantages, disadvantages and applications? 10

(b) What is GSM technology? Explain its advantages and disadvantages. 10

(c) What is a 4G network? Explain its features. 10

(d) What is WIMAX? Explain its features. 10

2. (a) What is Data Synchronization? Explain it. 10

(b) Write a short note on Mobile Commerce. 10

3. (a) Draw and explain Android architecture. 10

(b) Explain various components of J2ME. 10

4. (a) What is guided transmission? How does it differ from unguided transmission? Give example(s). 10

(b) Explain any two reasons for weakening of figural strength after transmission. 10

5. (a) What is an antenna? What is its functionality? On what factor(s) does its size depend on? 10

(b) What is CDMA? How does it differ from GSM? 10

Master In Computer Application (MCA)
Chapter 3: Term-End Examination, December, 2023
MCS-231: Mobile Computing

Time: 3 Hours
Maximum Marks:100
Note: Question No. 1 is compulsory and carries 40 marks. Attempt any three questions from the rest.

1. (a) What is Time Division Multiplexing (TDM)? What are its advantages, disadvantages and applications? 10

(b) What is a Cellular Network? Under what conditions frequency reuse is possible by different cells in the network? 10

(c) What are Smart Sensors? What are the instances where mobile devices interact with their surroundings with the help of sensors? 10

(d) Write a short note on Mobile Device Database Management. 10

2. (a) List various steps in the development of a Mobile App. What are the various components of an Enterprise Mobile Application? 10

(b) Write a short note on XML. 10

3. (a) What is J2ME? Explain main components of J2ME. 10

(b) Write a short note on Android. 10

4. (a) Explain the features of integrated development platforms that are used for Mobile App development. 10

(b) Explain any five features of Mobile Communications. 10

5. (a) Explain the design considerations for Mobile Computing. 10

(b) Write a short note on Smart Appliances. 10

Chapter 4: Most Asked Questions Part-A

1. What is mobile computing, and why has it become essential in modern technology?
Answer: Mobile computing refers to technology enabling transmission of data, voice, and video via mobile devices without being connected physically to a network. It involves devices such as smartphones, tablets, laptops, and portable computers. Mobile computing has become essential today due to the increasing need for constant connectivity, mobility, and access to information anytime and anywhere. It supports real-time data access, enhancing productivity and responsiveness in professional settings. Moreover, it facilitates seamless communication, collaboration, and social interaction among users globally. The proliferation of cloud computing services and wireless technologies such as Wi-Fi, LTE, and 5G has further accelerated its significance, providing a robust infrastructure for mobile computing solutions.

2. Explain the concept of location-based services (LBS) in mobile computing.
Answer: Location-based services (LBS) are applications that utilize geographical positioning data to provide information or functionalities tailored specifically to a user's current location. In mobile computing, LBS rely primarily on technologies like GPS (Global Positioning System), Wi-Fi, cell towers, or Bluetooth beacons to determine a user's geographical coordinates. Common examples of LBS include navigation systems, social media location tagging, geotargeted advertising, and real-time tracking services. LBS enhances user experiences by offering personalized content and services relevant to their immediate surroundings. Businesses leverage location-based services to provide targeted marketing and improve customer engagement. Privacy and security concerns are critical in LBS due to sensitive location data usage, necessitating strong data protection and privacy practices.

3. Differentiate between mobile computing and wireless computing.
Answer: Mobile computing refers specifically to computing activities enabled through portable or mobile devices that users can carry, such as smartphones, tablets, and laptops. It emphasizes mobility and portability, allowing users access to computing resources irrespective of their physical location. Wireless computing, however, pertains strictly to computing over wireless networks and does not necessarily require mobility. It can involve stationary devices that connect wirelessly to networks via Wi-Fi or other wireless technologies. Thus, while all mobile computing involves wireless communication, wireless computing can exist independently without mobility, such as desktops connected to wireless networks. Mobile computing emphasizes portability, whereas wireless computing emphasizes communication without wired connections.

4. How has the evolution from 3G to 5G impacted mobile computing?
Answer: The transition from 3G to 5G significantly transformed mobile computing capabilities by dramatically improving network speeds, reducing latency, and increasing reliability and connectivity. 3G provided basic internet capabilities, facilitating mobile browsing, emails, and limited multimedia services. With 4G LTE, data rates increased significantly, supporting HD video streaming, online gaming, and real-time applications. The arrival of 5G marked a revolutionary leap, offering ultra-fast data transfer speeds (up to several gigabits per second), minimal latency (around 1 millisecond), and the capability to handle a vast number of connected devices simultaneously. This advancement enabled real-time augmented reality (AR), virtual reality (VR), extensive IoT applications, autonomous vehicles, and unprecedented efficiency in mobile cloud computing services.

5. Describe the components of mobile computing architecture.
Answer: Mobile computing architecture consists primarily of three components: mobile devices, middleware, and network infrastructure. The mobile device component includes smartphones, tablets, PDAs, and laptops capable of wireless communication. Middleware comprises software that enables smooth communication between mobile devices and backend systems, handling issues such as data synchronization, security, context-awareness, and resource management. Examples include mobile databases, synchronization protocols, and APIs. The network infrastructure consists of wireless network technologies like Wi-Fi, Bluetooth, LTE, and 5G, providing connectivity and supporting communication between mobile devices and servers. Together, these components enable users to access applications and data anytime, anywhere, supporting seamless communication, application mobility, and uninterrupted access to information.

6. What is context-aware computing in mobile applications?
Answer: Context-aware computing refers to mobile applications' ability to adapt behaviors based on contextual information, such as the user's location, time, identity, activity, environmental conditions, or device status. In mobile computing, this involves sensing and interpreting context through sensors like GPS, accelerometers, gyroscopes, proximity sensors, and

ambient light sensors. Applications leverage context-awareness to deliver personalized and relevant experiences. For example, a smartphone automatically silencing notifications during meetings or recommending nearby restaurants at lunchtime illustrates context-aware computing. This capability significantly enhances usability, convenience, and efficiency, enabling proactive, user-centric interactions. The major challenge remains effectively interpreting context accurately while managing user privacy and data security.

7. Discuss the role of middleware in mobile computing.
Answer: Middleware in mobile computing serves as a critical intermediary layer between mobile applications and underlying systems such as operating systems, databases, and network infrastructures. It handles complexities like communication protocols, data management, security, resource allocation, and synchronization, allowing developers to focus on core application functionalities rather than low-level operations. Middleware enables seamless integration and interoperability among diverse mobile systems and backend resources, addressing challenges related to intermittent connectivity, bandwidth limitations, and heterogeneous devices. By simplifying application development, middleware accelerates deployment and improves maintainability. It also enhances security and scalability by providing standardized interfaces, authentication mechanisms, encryption services, and efficient resource utilization.

8. What challenges are associated with mobile computing security?
Answer: Mobile computing security involves numerous challenges, including device theft or loss, unauthorized data access, malware threats, insecure network connections, privacy vulnerabilities, and insufficient user awareness. Mobile devices are particularly susceptible to theft or misplacement, leading to risks of data breaches. Furthermore, mobile platforms can be targets of malware, spyware, and ransomware, exploiting vulnerabilities through malicious applications or phishing attacks. Wireless communication channels may expose data to interception or man-in-the-middle attacks. The heterogeneous nature of devices and operating systems complicates implementing uniform security standards. Addressing these issues requires comprehensive approaches involving strong authentication, encryption, secure communication protocols, regular security updates, user education, and robust enterprise security policies.

9. Define mobile cloud computing (MCC). How does it benefit users and enterprises?
Answer: Mobile Cloud Computing (MCC) integrates cloud computing with mobile computing, allowing mobile devices to access computational resources, storage, and services hosted remotely on the cloud. MCC overcomes mobile devices' inherent limitations, such as limited processing power, storage capacity, battery life, and bandwidth constraints. Users benefit significantly through enhanced application performance, data synchronization across devices, reduced local storage needs, and extended battery life. Enterprises leverage MCC to provide scalable, cost-effective, and reliable mobile services, improve collaboration, enhance productivity, and facilitate real-time data access. Moreover, MCC allows rapid deployment of services, streamlined maintenance, and simplified software updates, enhancing the agility and competitiveness of businesses adopting mobile cloud solutions.

10. What is meant by mobile device management (MDM), and why is it crucial for enterprises?
Answer: Mobile Device Management (MDM) involves software solutions designed to monitor, secure, manage, and support mobile devices deployed within an enterprise environment. It ensures devices comply with organizational policies, maintains device security, manages applications, tracks usage, and remotely controls devices in case of loss or security compromise. MDM solutions are crucial because they address critical enterprise concerns like data protection, unauthorized access prevention, and regulatory compliance, especially in BYOD (Bring Your Own Device) scenarios. It simplifies device provisioning, application distribution, and device tracking while enabling remote locking or wiping of devices when necessary. Thus, MDM enhances enterprise security, reduces operational risks, and improves overall productivity and management efficiency.

11. Explain the concept of Bring Your Own Device (BYOD) and its implications in mobile computing.
Answer: Bring Your Own Device (BYOD) refers to a corporate policy allowing employees to use their personal mobile devices such as smartphones, tablets, or laptops to access and work with corporate resources. BYOD offers numerous benefits, including cost savings for organizations, increased employee productivity, enhanced job satisfaction, and flexibility. However, it also introduces security risks, such as data breaches, unauthorized access, and difficulties managing diverse device types and operating systems. Enterprises adopting BYOD must address these challenges through robust policies, strict device management, stringent security measures like encryption and authentication, and employee training to mitigate potential vulnerabilities, ensuring both productivity and security within mobile computing environments.

12. What is mobile commerce (m-commerce), and how has it changed consumer behavior?

Answer: Mobile commerce (m-commerce) refers to the buying and selling of goods and services through wireless handheld devices, particularly smartphones and tablets. It includes activities like mobile banking, digital payments, mobile shopping, and online booking via mobile applications. M-commerce has significantly transformed consumer behavior by enabling instant access, convenience, and real-time transactions regardless of geographical location. Consumers increasingly prefer mobile shopping due to ease, personalized experiences, targeted marketing, and instant notifications. Businesses also leverage m-commerce for direct consumer engagement, improved customer loyalty, and insights through data analytics. However, challenges like secure transactions, privacy protection, and network reliability must be continuously managed to sustain consumer trust.

13. Describe the importance of mobile user interface (UI) design.
Answer: Mobile user interface (UI) design is critically important in ensuring usability, engagement, and satisfaction for mobile applications. Effective UI design accommodates mobile devices' limited screen sizes, varied resolutions, touch interaction, and diverse user environments. A well-designed UI simplifies navigation, reduces user errors, and enhances intuitiveness through clear visuals, logical flows, responsive gestures, and accessible features. Good UI design prioritizes user-centric elements like readability, consistency, immediate feedback, and accessibility, significantly improving user experience and increasing user retention rates. Poor UI design leads to frustration, low productivity, and higher abandonment rates. Thus, designing intuitive, visually appealing, and responsive mobile UI directly influences an application's success and user adoption.

14. What role does Bluetooth technology play in mobile computing?
Answer: Bluetooth is a wireless communication technology used for short-range data exchange between fixed and mobile devices. Within mobile computing, Bluetooth facilitates seamless connectivity and interoperability, enabling peripherals such as headphones, smartwatches, keyboards, mice, and speakers to connect wirelessly with mobile devices. Bluetooth supports low power consumption, making it ideal for battery-operated devices. Its low-energy variant (Bluetooth LE) is essential in IoT environments, wearables, and sensor-based applications. Bluetooth significantly enhances the mobile experience by simplifying device pairing, eliminating cables, and allowing convenient device interaction. Challenges with Bluetooth technology include limited transmission range, interference issues, and security vulnerabilities, necessitating proper configuration, pairing protocols, and encryption to safeguard communications.

15. How does mobile computing support disaster management?
Answer: Mobile computing significantly enhances disaster management by providing instant communication, real-time data collection, and rapid dissemination of crucial information during emergencies. Mobile devices equipped with GPS facilitate accurate location tracking and emergency response coordination. Applications designed specifically for disaster management support tasks such as early warnings, resource allocation, reporting incidents, and disseminating instructions to affected populations. Mobile computing infrastructure also helps authorities maintain connectivity when conventional communication networks fail, supporting coordination among rescue teams. Additionally, leveraging social media and messaging platforms through mobile devices enables effective communication with the public. However, managing power resources, network reliability, and robust security are essential to ensure continuous mobile computing effectiveness during disaster scenarios.

16. Define mobile IP and its importance in mobile computing.
Answer: Mobile IP is a standardized protocol developed to allow mobile devices to seamlessly maintain ongoing internet connectivity while moving between different network segments. It ensures continuous network access by assigning two IP addresses—a permanent home address and a temporary care-of address. Mobile IP routes data transparently, ensuring persistent connectivity without dropping sessions or losing communication when switching networks. This capability is crucial in mobile computing environments where mobility is fundamental, enabling devices like smartphones and laptops to maintain uninterrupted network sessions despite location changes. Mobile IP supports applications requiring persistent connectivity, such as streaming media, teleconferencing, and real-time applications, enhancing productivity and user experience across various mobile computing scenarios.

17. Explain the concept and challenges of Mobile Ad Hoc Networks (MANETs).
Answer: Mobile Ad Hoc Networks (MANETs) are decentralized, self-configuring networks of mobile devices interconnected wirelessly without predefined infrastructure. Devices in MANETs dynamically form networks, manage routing, and exchange data directly or through intermediary nodes. MANETs are ideal for scenarios requiring rapid network deployment, such as military operations, disaster recovery, and remote communication. However, MANETs face challenges, including dynamic topology management, limited battery life, bandwidth constraints, frequent network partitioning, security vulnerabilities, and efficient routing. Addressing these issues involves specialized routing protocols like AODV or DSR, secure data encryption

methods, power-efficient algorithms, and adaptive techniques ensuring stable and secure network communication in unpredictable, mobile environments.

18. Discuss the significance of Android and iOS in mobile computing.
Answer: Android and iOS are the dominant operating systems in mobile computing, significantly shaping the mobile technology landscape. Android, developed by Google, is open-source, customizable, and widely adopted across numerous devices globally, offering flexibility for developers and users. Its vast user base and open ecosystem enable diverse application availability and device affordability. iOS, developed by Apple, emphasizes high security, stability, performance consistency, and a seamless user experience, supported by a tightly controlled app ecosystem. Both operating systems drive innovation, extensive application development, and robust ecosystems supporting mobile computing. Their importance lies in standardizing app development, facilitating digital commerce, ensuring secure environments, and influencing consumer and developer behaviors across global mobile markets.

19. What is the significance of responsive web design in mobile computing?
Answer: Responsive web design ensures web pages adapt automatically to different screen sizes, resolutions, and orientations, providing optimal viewing experiences across various mobile devices. Its significance in mobile computing arises from the proliferation of diverse devices and screen types, enabling content accessibility and usability irrespective of hardware constraints. Responsive design eliminates the need for separate websites for mobile and desktop users, streamlining development and maintenance. It enhances user experience by ensuring content readability, reducing zooming or scrolling difficulties, and improving website performance and load times. Implementing responsive design increases user engagement, boosts search rankings, and drives higher conversion rates, making it a critical element for mobile-friendly, effective web strategies.

20. Describe wearable computing and its impact on mobile computing.
Answer: Wearable computing refers to electronic devices worn directly on the user's body, such as smartwatches, fitness bands, smart glasses, and health-monitoring devices, integrating seamlessly with mobile computing technologies. Wearables significantly impact mobile computing by enabling continuous data collection, real-time monitoring, and convenient interaction without interrupting user activities. They expand mobile computing capabilities through context-awareness, health tracking, fitness monitoring, and personalized notifications. Wearables drive the integration of mobile computing into everyday life, improving healthcare, productivity, communication, and lifestyle management. Challenges include privacy, battery life, data accuracy, and user acceptance. Overcoming these issues ensures seamless interaction between wearables and mobile devices, revolutionizing personal computing and expanding mobile computing horizons.

21. What is mobile virtualization in mobile computing?
Answer: Mobile virtualization refers to technology enabling multiple operating systems or virtual environments to run simultaneously on a single mobile device. It allows distinct separation between personal and business applications, enhancing security and manageability. Virtualization optimizes hardware utilization and reduces device costs by consolidating tasks traditionally requiring multiple devices. It improves device efficiency, ensures security through isolation, and facilitates enterprise mobility management. Challenges include performance overhead, limited battery resources, complexity in managing multiple environments, and potential compatibility issues. Nonetheless, mobile virtualization significantly aids organizations in securing corporate data while supporting Bring Your Own Device (BYOD) policies by efficiently managing multiple user profiles on a single device.

22. Define pervasive computing and its relationship with mobile computing.
Answer: Pervasive computing, also called ubiquitous computing, integrates computing capabilities seamlessly into everyday objects and environments, making technology indistinguishable from daily life. It ensures continuous availability of computing services regardless of user location or activity. Mobile computing relates closely as it provides the foundational technology enabling users to access computing resources on-the-go. Both concepts aim to provide seamless connectivity and intuitive user experiences. However, pervasive computing emphasizes invisibility and integration into the environment, whereas mobile computing emphasizes portability and mobility of computing devices. Together, they create an interconnected world where technology becomes an intuitive and invisible aspect of daily life, continuously enhancing convenience, productivity, and user interaction.

23. What are push notifications in mobile applications?
Answer: Push notifications are messages sent from a mobile application's server directly to the user's device without requiring explicit request from the user. These notifications inform users about new events, updates, reminders, or promotional offers,

enhancing user engagement. Push notifications leverage network protocols such as APNs for iOS or FCM for Android, delivering real-time alerts even when the application isn't active. They significantly increase user retention and activity within apps by providing timely, relevant information. Challenges involve user privacy, permission management, and avoiding notification overload, requiring careful strategy and user-centric approaches. Effective push notifications significantly improve application usability, customer interaction, and overall app experience.

24. How does Near Field Communication (NFC) function in mobile computing?
Answer: Near Field Communication (NFC) enables short-range wireless data transmission between devices when placed within centimeters of each other. NFC facilitates secure, quick communication, extensively used for contactless payments, ticketing, device pairing, and information exchange. Mobile computing leverages NFC to enable convenient mobile wallets, secure authentication, and simplified pairing between smartphones and peripherals. NFC tags embedded in physical objects provide context-sensitive information directly to mobile devices, enhancing user experiences. While NFC simplifies interactions, security vulnerabilities and limited range pose challenges. However, its secure communication through encryption and convenience for rapid transactions makes NFC integral to mobile computing ecosystems, significantly streamlining daily activities and transactions.

25. What is mobile synchronization, and why is it important?
Answer: Mobile synchronization refers to the automatic updating of data across multiple devices or servers, ensuring consistency and accuracy of information. It allows seamless access and continuity, regardless of the device or location. Synchronization covers contacts, emails, calendars, documents, photos, and application data, improving user convenience and productivity. Its importance lies in ensuring users always access the latest data, preventing conflicts, and minimizing data loss. Enterprises leverage synchronization for collaborative workflows and efficient resource management. Challenges include managing data conflicts, bandwidth limitations, and maintaining security during data transfers. Proper synchronization strategies ensure seamless user experiences, enhanced productivity, and reliable data availability across diverse mobile computing environments.

26. What is meant by "handoff" in mobile computing?
Answer: Handoff, also known as handover, refers to the process by which an active mobile connection seamlessly transitions from one base station or access point to another without interrupting the ongoing session. It occurs as users move between different coverage areas within cellular or wireless networks. Effective handoff ensures continuous connectivity, quality of service (QoS), and uninterrupted communication or data transfer. Challenges include managing latency, minimizing dropped connections, and ensuring efficient resource allocation during transitions. Proper implementation of handoff techniques, such as soft and hard handoffs, significantly enhances mobile network reliability and user experience, essential for real-time applications and consistent connectivity.

27. Explain mobile middleware's role in supporting disconnected operations.
Answer: Mobile middleware facilitates disconnected operations by enabling mobile applications to function effectively even without continuous network connectivity. It handles local data storage, caching, synchronization, and manages application behavior during intermittent network availability. Middleware ensures that data is cached locally when connectivity is available and intelligently synchronizes with servers once connectivity resumes. This approach enhances user experience, productivity, and application reliability, particularly in scenarios where network connectivity is unpredictable or unstable. Challenges include managing data consistency, handling conflicts during synchronization, and resource optimization. Effective middleware solutions ensure applications remain responsive, consistent, and operational, providing seamless user experiences regardless of temporary or prolonged disconnections in mobile computing environments.

28. What is the significance of energy-efficient protocols in mobile computing?
Answer: Energy-efficient protocols in mobile computing are designed to optimize power consumption, significantly extending battery life for mobile devices. These protocols carefully manage data transmission, network usage, processing load, and resource allocation to minimize energy usage. Techniques include sleep scheduling, data aggregation, efficient routing, and power-aware computation. Given the limited battery capacity of mobile devices, implementing these protocols ensures prolonged operational periods, enhancing user satisfaction and productivity. Energy-efficient protocols are crucial in IoT environments, wearables, and mobile ad hoc networks where constant recharging is impractical. Challenges include balancing energy savings against performance needs, highlighting the importance of energy efficiency to the effectiveness and longevity of mobile computing solutions.

29. Describe the role of mobile agents in mobile computing.
Answer: Mobile agents are autonomous software programs capable of moving independently across networks to execute tasks on behalf of users. They significantly enhance mobile computing by reducing network traffic, latency, and dependency on continuous connectivity. Mobile agents operate independently of user devices, handling tasks such as data retrieval, filtering, or processing remotely before returning results. This optimizes resource utilization, enhances performance, and reduces bandwidth requirements. Challenges include ensuring security, reliability, and managing agent mobility efficiently. Despite these complexities, mobile agents provide scalable solutions, promote fault-tolerance, and improve application responsiveness, offering significant advantages in mobile computing environments where network availability and bandwidth are limited or unpredictable.

30. Explain adaptive content delivery in mobile computing.
Answer: Adaptive content delivery in mobile computing involves dynamically adjusting digital content based on user context, device capabilities, network conditions, and preferences. This adaptation optimizes performance and user experience by modifying data formats, resolutions, quality, or interfaces suitable for mobile constraints such as limited bandwidth, screen size, and processing capabilities. Techniques include content transcoding, image optimization, adaptive streaming, and context-aware data delivery. Adaptive content delivery ensures efficient utilization of network resources, improves application responsiveness, and significantly enhances user satisfaction and engagement. Challenges include accurately identifying user context, balancing content quality with resource constraints, and managing real-time adaptation. Proper implementation ensures optimal mobile user experiences across diverse scenarios.

31. What is the role of GPS technology in mobile computing?
Answer: GPS (Global Positioning System) technology provides precise geographic location information to mobile computing devices, enabling location-based services, navigation, tracking, and real-time mapping. It helps users in activities such as route guidance, vehicle tracking, geotagging, emergency services, and targeted advertising. GPS significantly improves the contextual relevance of mobile applications by providing accurate, real-time location data. Integration of GPS with mobile computing enables enhanced personalization, efficiency, and productivity. Challenges with GPS include battery consumption, reduced accuracy in densely populated urban environments, and privacy concerns related to location tracking. Despite these issues, GPS remains essential for developing innovative, user-centric applications across various mobile computing scenarios.

32. What are mobile databases and their importance?
Answer: Mobile databases are specialized databases designed to operate effectively on mobile devices, supporting data storage, retrieval, and synchronization in a mobile computing environment. These databases allow data access even when disconnected from a network, caching information locally and synchronizing when connectivity is restored. Mobile databases significantly improve user experience by providing reliable offline access, reducing latency, and managing resource constraints effectively. They support enterprise mobility, enabling mobile workers to access and update information seamlessly. Challenges include synchronization conflicts, limited storage capacity, and data consistency management. Nevertheless, effective mobile database solutions improve application responsiveness, data availability, and productivity, making them vital in mobile computing.

33. How does mobile computing enhance education?
Answer: Mobile computing significantly enhances education by providing accessible, interactive, and personalized learning experiences through portable devices such as smartphones and tablets. It supports digital classrooms, distance learning, and mobile educational applications offering multimedia content, interactive lessons, quizzes, and real-time collaboration among students and educators. Mobile computing fosters flexible learning, allowing students to access educational resources anytime and anywhere, promoting active participation and improving engagement. Challenges include managing screen time, digital distraction, and ensuring equitable access to technology. Nonetheless, effective integration of mobile computing into education improves learning outcomes, increases knowledge retention, promotes inclusivity, and prepares learners for technology-driven environments in academic and professional spheres.

34. What is mobile application testing, and why is it essential?
Answer: Mobile application testing involves validating applications for functionality, performance, usability, security, and compatibility across various devices, operating systems, and network conditions. It ensures applications meet quality standards, provide positive user experiences, and function reliably under diverse scenarios. Essential aspects include functional testing, performance testing under varying network speeds, usability testing for intuitive interfaces, compatibility

testing on multiple device models, and security testing against vulnerabilities. Effective testing identifies issues early, reduces development costs, improves reliability, and ensures user satisfaction. Challenges include device fragmentation, rapid technology evolution, and complex user environments. Thorough testing is essential to deliver successful mobile applications capable of meeting user expectations and performance standards.

35. Define mobile crowdsensing and its applications.
Answer: Mobile crowdsensing involves collecting data from numerous mobile devices operated by users to measure, monitor, and analyze phenomena across diverse locations. Users contribute sensor data such as location, temperature, images, or noise levels through their smartphones, creating large-scale data collection platforms. Applications include traffic monitoring, environmental sensing, urban planning, public health monitoring, and disaster management. Crowdsensing leverages widespread device penetration, enabling cost-effective, real-time, and large-scale data collection. Challenges include ensuring user privacy, data accuracy, participation incentives, and managing large data volumes. Despite these issues, mobile crowdsensing provides valuable insights and improves decision-making processes in numerous applications benefiting communities and organizations worldwide.

36. How does mobile computing influence social networking?
Answer: Mobile computing significantly influences social networking by enabling constant connectivity, real-time communication, and location-based interactions through mobile devices. Users can access social media anytime and anywhere, sharing content instantly, engaging in real-time conversations, and leveraging location-aware services like check-ins and event tagging. Mobile computing has transformed social media dynamics, fostering instant communication, immediacy, and global reach. It supports personalized content delivery, enhances user engagement, and enables seamless multimedia sharing. Challenges include privacy risks, digital addiction, cyberbullying, and misinformation spread. Nevertheless, mobile computing's integration with social networking has profoundly changed social interactions, increased global connectivity, and reshaped communication patterns across societies and cultures.

37. What is wireless application protocol (WAP) in mobile computing?
Answer: Wireless Application Protocol (WAP) is a standardized protocol enabling mobile devices to access internet content specifically optimized for mobile environments. It facilitates communication between mobile devices and web servers, translating standard web pages into formats suitable for limited bandwidth, small screens, and constrained processing power of mobile devices. WAP introduced the concept of mobile web browsing, offering services like email access, news updates, and basic information retrieval before modern mobile browsers emerged. Challenges included limited multimedia support, slow data rates, and user interface limitations. Though replaced by advanced technologies like HTML5, WAP played a crucial role historically in pioneering internet connectivity and mobile web services for early mobile devices.

38. Explain the concept of mobile health (mHealth).
Answer: Mobile health (mHealth) involves using mobile devices and wireless technologies to provide healthcare services, medical information, patient monitoring, and remote consultations. It encompasses applications for health tracking, telemedicine, medication reminders, disease management, and preventive care. mHealth significantly improves healthcare accessibility, efficiency, and patient engagement by enabling remote patient monitoring, reducing hospital visits, and facilitating continuous health management. Challenges include ensuring data privacy, accuracy of health information, and equitable access. Nevertheless, mHealth solutions enhance healthcare delivery, reduce healthcare costs, improve patient outcomes, and enable personalized healthcare management, significantly transforming healthcare services and expanding healthcare access in resource-constrained and remote areas globally.

39. Describe mobile analytics and its importance in mobile computing.
Answer: Mobile analytics involves collecting, measuring, and analyzing data from mobile applications and users to understand user behavior, preferences, performance metrics, and application usage patterns. It provides insights into user demographics, engagement levels, application usage frequency, retention rates, and effectiveness of marketing campaigns. Mobile analytics is crucial for improving application performance, optimizing user experiences, increasing user retention, and maximizing revenue through targeted advertising and content personalization. Challenges include ensuring user privacy, data security, and managing large data volumes effectively. Proper utilization of analytics enables informed decision-making, improved marketing strategies, and continuous application improvement, significantly enhancing user satisfaction, competitiveness, and success in mobile computing ecosystems.

40. What is augmented reality (AR), and how is it utilized in mobile computing?
Answer: Augmented Reality (AR) overlays digital information or virtual elements onto real-world environments, enhancing user perception and interaction through mobile devices like smartphones or tablets. Mobile computing enables AR applications such as navigation, gaming, education, retail experiences, and real-time information overlays. AR significantly enriches user experiences by providing interactive, immersive, and contextually relevant content. For instance, AR applications enhance education through interactive lessons, improve shopping experiences through virtual try-ons, and assist navigation through real-time visual guidance. Challenges include hardware constraints, battery consumption, and content accuracy. Nonetheless, AR technology significantly expands mobile computing capabilities, driving innovation across various industries and improving user engagement and experiences substantially.

41. Define mobile backend as a service (MBaaS).
Answer: Mobile Backend as a Service (MBaaS) provides developers with cloud-based backend infrastructure to support mobile applications. MBaaS manages essential backend tasks such as user authentication, data storage, database management, push notifications, and analytics. It simplifies mobile app development by eliminating the need for developers to build and maintain server-side functionalities from scratch. MBaaS significantly accelerates development cycles, reduces time-to-market, and ensures scalability. Popular examples include Firebase and AWS Amplify. Challenges involve dependency on service providers, potential vendor lock-in, and limited control over infrastructure. Nevertheless, MBaaS streamlines mobile development processes, reduces costs, and allows developers to focus primarily on front-end features and user experience.

42. What is mobile payment security, and why is it crucial?
Answer: Mobile payment security encompasses protective measures employed to ensure safe and secure financial transactions through mobile devices. It includes encryption, tokenization, biometric authentication, secure protocols, and fraud detection mechanisms. Mobile payment security prevents unauthorized access, fraud, and theft of sensitive financial data, safeguarding users and businesses from monetary losses and reputational damage. As mobile transactions rise, robust security is vital for consumer trust and widespread adoption. Challenges involve managing threats like phishing, malware, data breaches, and securing user privacy without compromising convenience. Strong security practices are essential to maintain user confidence, promote mobile payment usage, and support ongoing growth in mobile commerce and digital financial transactions.

43. How does mobile computing benefit enterprise resource planning (ERP)?
Answer: Mobile computing significantly enhances Enterprise Resource Planning (ERP) by providing real-time data access, improved decision-making, and greater operational efficiency through mobile ERP applications. Employees access essential business processes, inventory management, sales updates, financial data, and customer interactions remotely, leading to quicker responses and enhanced productivity. Mobile ERP improves collaboration across departments, facilitates accurate data capture at points-of-activity, and reduces processing delays. Challenges include data synchronization, security risks, user interface limitations, and maintaining seamless integration across enterprise systems. Despite these challenges, effective mobile ERP solutions optimize business processes, improve resource management, and enhance organizational agility, giving enterprises a competitive advantage in fast-paced business environments.

44. Explain the concept of mobile context modeling.
Answer: Mobile context modeling involves capturing and representing contextual information such as user location, time, activities, preferences, and device capabilities to enhance application interactions and user experience. Context models use sensor data, user inputs, and historical interactions to predict user needs and adapt application behaviors proactively. For example, context models enable applications to suggest nearby restaurants during lunchtime or switch device profiles during meetings. Effective modeling significantly enhances personalization, reduces user effort, and improves application usability. Challenges include accurately interpreting context, maintaining privacy, and handling ambiguous situations. Despite these challenges, robust context modeling significantly improves mobile application responsiveness and relevance, enhancing user satisfaction and engagement.

45. What are mobile operating systems, and why are they essential?
Answer: Mobile operating systems (OS) are software platforms specifically designed to operate smartphones, tablets, and other mobile devices. They manage hardware resources, provide application execution environments, ensure security, and facilitate user-device interaction through intuitive interfaces. Major examples include Android and iOS. Mobile operating systems are essential as they standardize device interactions, ensure application compatibility, enable seamless multitasking, and manage power efficiency. They significantly influence user experiences, device security, and application ecosystem development. Challenges include security vulnerabilities, device fragmentation, and maintaining consistency across diverse

hardware. Effective mobile OS solutions underpin user satisfaction, promote application innovation, enhance device performance, and support the extensive growth of mobile computing environments globally.

46. What is mobile edge computing (MEC)?
Answer: Mobile Edge Computing (MEC) involves deploying computing resources, storage, and networking capabilities at the network edge near mobile users, reducing latency and improving response times for mobile applications. MEC supports applications demanding real-time performance, such as augmented reality, virtual reality, IoT, and autonomous vehicles, by processing data locally rather than in distant cloud servers. MEC significantly improves user experiences, reduces network congestion, and enhances data privacy by processing sensitive data closer to users. Challenges include infrastructure deployment, resource management, and integration complexity. Nevertheless, MEC optimizes network performance, ensures high-speed interactions, and provides crucial support for latency-sensitive applications, significantly enhancing mobile computing's effectiveness, responsiveness, and overall user satisfaction.

47. What are QR codes, and how are they used in mobile computing?
Answer: Quick Response (QR) codes are two-dimensional barcodes capable of storing digital information accessible by scanning with mobile device cameras. QR codes facilitate mobile computing by providing rapid, seamless access to websites, payment gateways, contact information, product details, and promotional content without manual data entry. Mobile users scan QR codes using smartphones, instantly accessing relevant digital content or initiating transactions. QR codes simplify interactions, improve convenience, and significantly enhance user experiences, particularly in marketing, retail, ticketing, and payments. Challenges include ensuring secure scanning, protecting against malicious content, and user awareness. Nonetheless, QR codes significantly streamline mobile interactions, driving user engagement, convenience, and digital transaction efficiency.

48. How do sensors enhance mobile computing?
Answer: Sensors embedded in mobile devices significantly enhance mobile computing by providing real-time data about user context, environment, and device orientation. Common sensors include GPS, accelerometers, gyroscopes, proximity sensors, ambient light sensors, and biometric sensors. They enable applications to adapt dynamically, providing personalized experiences based on user activity, location, health status, or environmental conditions. Sensors facilitate functionalities like navigation, health monitoring, fitness tracking, gaming interactions, context-aware notifications, and augmented reality experiences. Challenges involve ensuring sensor accuracy, managing battery consumption, and protecting user privacy. Despite these challenges, sensors greatly expand the capabilities of mobile computing, enabling smarter, context-aware applications that significantly improve user interactions and experiences.

49. Explain mobile network operators (MNOs) in mobile computing.
Answer: Mobile Network Operators (MNOs) provide wireless communication services to users through cellular networks. They manage infrastructure such as base stations, towers, and networking equipment, enabling mobile connectivity for voice, data, and messaging. MNOs offer various services, including mobile broadband, roaming, SMS, MMS, and internet access. They play a crucial role in mobile computing by ensuring connectivity, supporting mobile application functionality, and facilitating real-time communication and data transmission. Challenges include managing network capacity, ensuring quality-of-service, and implementing secure network access. Effective operation by MNOs is essential to mobile computing's performance, reliability, and scalability, underpinning the connectivity necessary for seamless user experiences and efficient mobile applications globally.

50. Define session mobility in mobile computing.
Answer: Session mobility in mobile computing refers to maintaining active sessions or ongoing interactions seamlessly as users switch between devices, networks, or locations without disrupting service continuity. It ensures persistent access to resources, maintaining the session state regardless of the user's mobility. Session mobility supports continuous operations for applications like video conferencing, online gaming, streaming media, and cloud services. Challenges include handling network latency, seamless session transfer, maintaining data integrity, and security during transitions. Effective session mobility significantly enhances user experiences, productivity, and application reliability by ensuring uninterrupted interactions and data availability, enabling users to seamlessly switch devices or networks while maintaining continuous, stable connections and interactions.

51. What is meant by cellular frequency reuse in mobile computing?
Answer: Cellular frequency reuse refers to the strategic reuse of frequency bands within a cellular network to efficiently utilize limited radio spectrum resources. It involves dividing the geographic service area into cells, assigning frequencies, and

systematically reusing these frequencies in non-adjacent cells. This method increases capacity, reduces interference, and supports a greater number of simultaneous users within the network. Frequency reuse significantly improves spectrum efficiency, enhances network coverage, and ensures higher-quality communication. Challenges include managing interference between adjacent cells, optimizing cell size, and frequency planning complexities. Effective frequency reuse planning is crucial in providing reliable mobile communication services, improving network capacity, and accommodating growing demand in mobile computing environments.

52. Explain the significance of HTML5 in mobile computing.
Answer: HTML5 significantly impacts mobile computing by providing a standardized markup language optimized for multimedia, interactive web applications, and cross-platform compatibility. HTML5 enables developers to create responsive websites and mobile web apps without relying heavily on device-specific platforms or proprietary technologies. It supports multimedia elements (audio, video), offline storage, geolocation, and improved user interactions. HTML5 ensures broader accessibility across different browsers and devices, significantly enhancing the user experience. Challenges include varying browser implementations, performance optimization, and compatibility issues with legacy devices. Despite these issues, HTML5 simplifies mobile web development, reduces dependency on native apps, and supports richer, more interactive, and platform-independent mobile experiences.

53. Describe the impact of voice recognition technology in mobile computing.
Answer: Voice recognition technology transforms mobile computing by enabling users to interact hands-free, issuing voice commands, dictating messages, performing searches, and accessing applications using natural speech. It significantly improves accessibility, convenience, and user engagement, especially while driving or multitasking. Popularized by assistants like Siri, Google Assistant, and Alexa, voice recognition simplifies device interaction, enhancing usability and efficiency. Challenges include accurately interpreting accents, handling ambient noise, ensuring user privacy, and managing processing resources. Despite these challenges, advancements in voice recognition have profoundly improved mobile device accessibility, facilitated personalized experiences, and significantly reshaped user interactions, driving further adoption and innovation in mobile computing applications worldwide.

54. Define Geofencing and its applications in mobile computing.
Answer: Geofencing involves creating virtual geographic boundaries using GPS or RFID technology, triggering specific actions when mobile devices enter, exit, or remain within defined areas. In mobile computing, geofencing supports location-based notifications, targeted advertising, security alerts, and monitoring applications. For example, retailers use geofencing to send promotions to nearby customers, and security apps utilize geofencing to alert when devices leave specified areas. Geofencing significantly enhances user engagement, security, and operational efficiency. Challenges include maintaining precise boundary accuracy, managing battery consumption, and addressing privacy concerns. Nevertheless, geofencing effectively delivers contextual relevance, improves customer interactions, ensures safety, and supports innovative location-aware mobile services across diverse application domains.

55. What are the challenges of integrating mobile computing with cloud computing?
Answer: Integrating mobile computing with cloud computing involves several challenges, including network latency, data synchronization, security, privacy, energy constraints, and bandwidth limitations. Latency affects application responsiveness and user experience due to distant cloud servers. Data synchronization issues arise from intermittent connectivity and data conflicts across multiple devices. Security and privacy concerns stem from sensitive data transmission and storage on cloud servers. Additionally, mobile devices' limited battery life constrains heavy data processing and frequent synchronization activities. Effective integration requires addressing these challenges through edge computing, efficient synchronization protocols, robust security mechanisms, and energy-efficient communication strategies. Successful integration ensures seamless user experiences, improved performance, scalability, and reliable access to cloud resources.

56. What is meant by mobile streaming, and why is it significant?
Answer: Mobile streaming refers to delivering continuous multimedia content like audio or video in real-time to mobile devices over wireless networks without needing full prior download. Streaming significantly enhances user experience by providing immediate playback, reducing wait times, and optimizing bandwidth usage. It enables live broadcasts, video conferencing, on-demand media consumption, and interactive services. The growing popularity of platforms like YouTube, Netflix, and Spotify highlights mobile streaming's importance, driven by increased mobile network speeds and improved data compression techniques. However, challenges include network congestion, buffering, latency, and maintaining consistent quality. Effective streaming technologies ensure smooth, uninterrupted media experiences, supporting user satisfaction and driving mobile media consumption growth.

57. Define mobile gaming and its impact on mobile computing.
Answer: Mobile gaming involves playing interactive digital games on portable devices such as smartphones and tablets. It significantly impacts mobile computing by driving technological advancements in graphics, processing power, user interfaces, and connectivity. Mobile gaming has popularized casual gaming, multiplayer interaction, and social integration through platforms like social media and messaging apps. The widespread adoption of mobile games stimulates innovation, content monetization, and new business models such as freemium and subscription services. Challenges include device compatibility, battery consumption, performance optimization, and managing digital addiction. Despite these issues, mobile gaming remains a major catalyst for growth, technological evolution, and consumer engagement within the broader ecosystem of mobile computing worldwide.

58. Explain the significance of device fragmentation in mobile computing.
Answer: Device fragmentation refers to the presence of multiple device models, screen sizes, operating systems, and hardware configurations within mobile computing environments. Fragmentation significantly complicates application development, testing, deployment, and maintenance, as developers must ensure compatibility and consistent experiences across diverse devices. Fragmentation poses challenges like increased development costs, longer time-to-market, varying performance levels, inconsistent user experiences, and complex testing scenarios. To mitigate fragmentation impacts, developers employ strategies like responsive design, cross-platform frameworks, and comprehensive device testing. Despite these challenges, managing fragmentation effectively ensures broader user reach, enhanced user satisfaction, and consistent application performance, essential for the sustainable growth of mobile computing applications across diverse user bases.

59. What is mobile remote access, and why is it important?
Answer: Mobile remote access enables users to securely connect to and control systems or resources located remotely from mobile devices. It supports tasks such as accessing corporate files, managing IT infrastructure, remote troubleshooting, and telecommuting. Mobile remote access significantly enhances productivity by providing flexibility, continuous availability, and efficient resource management irrespective of physical location. It empowers businesses by enabling mobile workforces, improving responsiveness, and reducing downtime. However, remote access poses security risks such as unauthorized access, data interception, and device vulnerabilities. Effective security measures like encryption, authentication, and VPNs are crucial. Proper implementation ensures secure, reliable remote connectivity, enhancing organizational agility, productivity, and operational efficiency in mobile computing scenarios.

60. Describe mobile instant messaging (IM) and its importance.
Answer: Mobile instant messaging (IM) refers to real-time text-based communication between users through mobile devices, facilitating rapid exchange of messages, multimedia content, and documents. Platforms like WhatsApp, Telegram, and Facebook Messenger exemplify mobile IM's widespread adoption. It significantly enhances communication efficiency, immediacy, and collaboration by providing instantaneous message delivery, read receipts, and group conversations. Mobile IM fosters continuous connectivity, supporting personal interactions and enterprise collaboration. Challenges include privacy issues, misinformation dissemination, and digital distractions. Nonetheless, mobile IM remains critical for efficient communication, facilitating both personal relationships and professional collaboration, underpinning global connectivity and engagement, and driving mobile computing's pervasive social integration.

61. Explain mobile biometric authentication and its role in security.
Answer: Mobile biometric authentication uses biological characteristics, such as fingerprints, facial recognition, voice patterns, or iris scans, to verify user identities on mobile devices. It significantly enhances security by providing reliable, convenient, and user-friendly methods for authentication, reducing dependence on passwords that are easily forgotten, stolen, or compromised. Biometric authentication ensures robust access control, safeguarding sensitive data, applications, and financial transactions. Challenges include managing biometric data securely, privacy concerns, and potential errors due to environmental factors or sensor inaccuracies. Nonetheless, biometric authentication significantly strengthens mobile security, ensuring user convenience, improving trust, and providing superior protection against unauthorized access, critical for secure mobile computing ecosystems.

62. What is mobile VPN, and why is it significant?
Answer: Mobile Virtual Private Network (VPN) provides secure, encrypted connections for mobile devices accessing networks remotely, ensuring data privacy, confidentiality, and integrity. It enables secure communication over public

Wi-Fi or cellular networks, protecting against interception, hacking, or eavesdropping. Mobile VPNs are essential for enterprise security, remote working, accessing geographically restricted content, and maintaining privacy. They facilitate seamless connectivity, continuous network access, and reliable data transmission, significantly enhancing user productivity and operational flexibility. Challenges include managing VPN overhead, maintaining connection stability, and user-friendly configurations. Effective mobile VPN solutions significantly contribute to secure mobile computing, ensuring reliable and confidential network access irrespective of geographic location, network security, or connection reliability.

63. Define mobile learning (mLearning) and its impact.
Answer: Mobile learning (mLearning) refers to educational practices leveraging mobile devices like smartphones and tablets to deliver educational content, resources, and interactive learning experiences. It significantly impacts education by facilitating flexible, personalized, and accessible learning, supporting anytime, anywhere educational access. mLearning enables interactive multimedia content, real-time communication, and collaborative learning experiences. It promotes continuous skill development, learner engagement, and educational inclusivity, bridging geographical and economic barriers. Challenges include ensuring equitable technology access, maintaining learner motivation, and avoiding digital distractions. Despite these, mLearning has transformed traditional education models, enabling lifelong learning, enhancing knowledge retention, and significantly expanding educational opportunities through pervasive mobile computing technologies.

64. What role does mobile computing play in the Internet of Things (IoT)?
Answer: Mobile computing significantly contributes to the Internet of Things (IoT) by providing interfaces, communication channels, and platforms for interacting with and managing IoT devices. Mobile devices serve as central controllers, collecting data, sending commands, and enabling user interaction with connected smart objects like wearables, smart home devices, and industrial sensors. Mobile computing ensures real-time monitoring, remote control, and data visualization, significantly enhancing user convenience and operational efficiency. Challenges include managing large data volumes, ensuring interoperability, and addressing security vulnerabilities. Despite these challenges, mobile computing remains crucial in IoT ecosystems, enabling user-friendly management, instant communication, and seamless integration across numerous smart devices, driving IoT adoption and innovation globally.

65. What is mobile CRM, and how does it improve customer relationships?
Answer: Mobile Customer Relationship Management (CRM) involves accessing and managing customer relationship data and interactions through mobile devices. It significantly enhances customer relationships by providing real-time access to customer information, history, and preferences remotely. Sales and customer service teams use mobile CRM to manage customer interactions effectively, respond promptly to inquiries, and improve personalized engagement. Mobile CRM supports informed decision-making, faster response times, improved customer satisfaction, and increased sales productivity. Challenges include maintaining data synchronization, ensuring security, and user interface usability. Effective implementation of mobile CRM significantly improves customer relationship management by enhancing responsiveness, personalization, and overall customer experience, thereby driving customer loyalty and business success in competitive markets.

66. What is the role of 5G technology in transforming mobile computing?
Answer: 5G technology is revolutionizing mobile computing by providing ultra-fast data speeds, significantly reduced latency, and support for massive device connectivity. These advancements allow real-time applications such as augmented reality (AR), virtual reality (VR), autonomous vehicles, and remote surgeries to perform efficiently. For mobile computing, 5G enhances user experiences through seamless video streaming, faster cloud access, and smoother IoT integration. It also enables edge computing, processing data closer to users for quicker responses. Challenges include infrastructure deployment costs, device compatibility, and security risks. Despite this, 5G is a foundational technology that will unlock new possibilities and accelerate innovations in mobile computing.

67. Explain the concept of mobile peer-to-peer (P2P) communication.
Answer: Mobile peer-to-peer (P2P) communication refers to the direct exchange of data or resources between mobile devices without relying on a centralized server or intermediary network. It enables sharing files, collaborating in real-time, and running distributed applications in a decentralized environment. Technologies like Wi-Fi Direct, Bluetooth, and ad hoc networks make mobile P2P possible. This communication model supports applications like mobile

payments, collaborative gaming, and disaster recovery systems where traditional networks may be unavailable. Challenges include security vulnerabilities, data synchronization issues, and scalability limitations. Mobile P2P communication enhances flexibility, reduces dependency on infrastructure, and fosters innovative mobile applications in dynamic environments.

68. How does mobile computing support smart cities?
Answer: Mobile computing is a critical enabler of smart cities by connecting citizens, services, and infrastructure through mobile devices and applications. It supports real-time traffic management, environmental monitoring, public safety systems, and efficient energy consumption. Mobile apps provide residents access to government services, transport updates, and emergency alerts. Sensors integrated with mobile networks help collect data to optimize urban planning and service delivery. Challenges include data privacy, network congestion, and ensuring equitable access. Mobile computing creates smarter, more sustainable urban ecosystems by empowering citizens, improving governance, and facilitating data-driven decision-making to enhance overall quality of life in smart cities.

69. What is mobile push technology, and how does it improve user engagement?
Answer: Mobile push technology delivers timely updates, alerts, or content directly to a user's device without requiring the user to request it actively. It keeps users informed about important events, promotions, or application activities, even when the app isn't open. Push notifications improve engagement by encouraging users to revisit apps, complete transactions, or interact with content. They are widely used in messaging apps, e-commerce platforms, and social media to drive activity and retention. However, excessive notifications may lead to user fatigue or app uninstalls. When implemented strategically, mobile push technology enhances communication, strengthens brand loyalty, and ensures users remain connected and informed.

70. Describe mobile blockchain applications and their significance.
Answer: Mobile blockchain applications integrate decentralized ledger technologies into mobile devices to offer secure, transparent, and tamper-proof transactions. These applications enable mobile payments, cryptocurrency trading, supply chain tracking, identity verification, and smart contracts. Blockchain enhances mobile security by removing centralized control and reducing risks of data breaches or fraud. For instance, mobile wallets use blockchain to facilitate secure digital currency transactions. Challenges include scalability, energy efficiency, and ensuring user-friendly designs for complex technologies. Despite these hurdles, blockchain on mobile devices empowers users with greater data ownership, fosters trust in transactions, and opens up innovative business models in financial, healthcare, and governance sectors.

71. What is mobile device tethering, and what are its uses?
Answer: Mobile device tethering enables a smartphone or tablet to share its internet connection with other devices such as laptops or tablets. It acts as a portable Wi-Fi hotspot using cellular data networks like 4G or 5G. Tethering is valuable for travelers, remote workers, or emergency situations where fixed internet access isn't available. It supports productivity and ensures seamless connectivity across multiple devices. Challenges include battery drain, high data consumption, and potential network provider restrictions. When used judiciously, tethering transforms mobile devices into essential connectivity tools, ensuring users maintain reliable internet access wherever traditional network infrastructure may be unavailable.

72. Explain the importance of power management in mobile computing devices.
Answer: Power management is vital in mobile computing devices to prolong battery life, enhance device performance, and reduce energy consumption. Mobile devices rely on limited power resources, and efficient power management ensures they can run applications, maintain connectivity, and deliver high performance without frequent recharging. Techniques include adaptive brightness, optimized background processing, energy-efficient hardware, and intelligent software algorithms. Developers also design power-aware applications that minimize unnecessary resource use. Challenges arise with energy-hungry applications, multitasking demands, and constant connectivity requirements. Effective power management supports longer usage times, user satisfaction, and sustainability, making it a crucial factor in designing mobile computing ecosystems.

73. What are the applications of RFID in mobile computing?
Answer: Radio-Frequency Identification (RFID) in mobile computing enables wireless tracking and identification of objects or people using electromagnetic fields. RFID tags store data that can be read by mobile devices equipped with

RFID readers. Applications include inventory management, contactless payments, asset tracking, supply chain automation, and access control systems. Mobile devices integrated with RFID capabilities enhance operational efficiency, reduce manual errors, and provide real-time visibility in various industries. Challenges involve security risks, data privacy concerns, and the cost of implementation. Despite these challenges, RFID integration with mobile computing fosters automation, improves accuracy, and supports smarter decision-making in dynamic business environments.

74. Define location-aware computing and its benefits.
Answer: Location-aware computing uses a mobile device's geographic position to deliver context-sensitive services, applications, or information tailored to the user's current location. Technologies like GPS, Wi-Fi positioning, and cellular triangulation enable location detection. Benefits include enhanced navigation, targeted advertising, personalized recommendations, and improved emergency response services. Businesses use location-awareness for geotargeted marketing and optimizing service delivery. Challenges include ensuring location accuracy, preserving user privacy, and managing battery consumption from continuous tracking. When implemented responsibly, location-aware computing significantly enhances user experiences, supports smarter applications, and enables innovative services that adapt dynamically to users' physical environments and needs.

75. What is mobile augmented commerce (m-commerce with AR), and how does it work?
Answer: Mobile augmented commerce combines m-commerce with augmented reality (AR) to provide immersive shopping experiences through smartphones and tablets. It allows users to visualize products in their physical environment before purchase, such as trying virtual furniture in their home or testing cosmetics on their face. AR-enabled m-commerce improves buyer confidence, reduces product returns, and enhances customer engagement. Retailers leverage AR to stand out in competitive markets and create interactive shopping experiences. Challenges include technical limitations, high development costs, and device compatibility. Despite these, mobile augmented commerce transforms traditional online shopping, offering innovative, engaging, and personalized retail solutions through mobile computing technologies.

76. How does artificial intelligence (AI) integrate with mobile computing?
Answer: Artificial intelligence (AI) integrates with mobile computing by enabling devices to perform intelligent tasks such as voice recognition, predictive text, image classification, and personalized recommendations. AI powers virtual assistants like Siri and Google Assistant, enabling natural language processing and contextual responses. It enhances mobile applications through features like chatbots, real-time translations, and adaptive user experiences. AI algorithms also optimize battery life, security, and app performance on mobile devices. Challenges include ensuring privacy, managing computational resource limitations, and avoiding biases in AI models. Despite these issues, AI integration in mobile computing has transformed user experiences, making devices smarter, more responsive, and highly personalized.

77. What is mobile forensics, and why is it important in cybersecurity?
Answer: Mobile forensics involves extracting, preserving, and analyzing data from mobile devices for use in investigations or legal proceedings. It plays a crucial role in cybersecurity by helping identify breaches, track unauthorized activities, and recover digital evidence after incidents like data theft or cyberattacks. Mobile forensics tools recover deleted messages, call logs, app data, and location history while maintaining data integrity. Challenges include encryption, device diversity, frequent OS updates, and ensuring evidence admissibility in court. Its importance lies in addressing cybercrime, enforcing security policies, and supporting law enforcement in tackling digital threats within the expanding landscape of mobile computing environments.

78. Explain the concept of zero-trust security in mobile computing.
Answer: Zero-trust security in mobile computing is an approach that assumes no user, device, or application should be trusted by default, even if within a secured network perimeter. Instead, it enforces strict verification for every access request, leveraging multifactor authentication, device posture checks, and continuous monitoring. In mobile computing, zero-trust protects data on devices that frequently connect to various networks, including unsecured public Wi-Fi. It reduces the risk of unauthorized access and data breaches by verifying identity and enforcing least-privilege access. Implementing zero-trust faces challenges like balancing security with user convenience. However, it is vital for safeguarding sensitive mobile data in today's highly dynamic environments.

79. What are progressive web apps (PWAs), and how do they support mobile computing?
Answer: Progressive Web Apps (PWAs) are web applications designed to provide app-like experiences on mobile devices using modern web technologies. PWAs combine the best of web and native apps, offering offline functionality, push notifications, and responsive design without requiring installation from app stores. They support mobile computing by enabling seamless user experiences across devices and platforms, with reduced storage and data usage. Businesses use PWAs to deliver fast, reliable, and engaging services accessible via browsers. Challenges include limited hardware access compared to native apps and varying browser support. PWAs enhance mobile computing by ensuring accessibility, faster load times, and broad reach for users.

80. How does mobile computing facilitate real-time collaboration?
Answer: Mobile computing facilitates real-time collaboration by enabling users to communicate, share files, and work together on tasks from any location using portable devices and internet connectivity. Tools like Slack, Microsoft Teams, and Google Workspace allow team members to co-edit documents, video conference, and track project progress simultaneously. This flexibility enhances productivity, reduces delays, and supports remote work environments. Mobile computing empowers organizations to operate efficiently across time zones and geographical boundaries. Challenges include ensuring secure data sharing, maintaining connectivity, and managing device compatibility. When implemented effectively, mobile collaboration transforms workflows, enhances decision-making, and supports agile, dynamic workforces in today's digital era.

81. What is mobile intrusion detection, and how does it protect devices?
Answer: Mobile intrusion detection refers to security systems designed to monitor mobile devices for suspicious activities, unauthorized access attempts, or malware. These systems detect anomalies in user behavior, application activity, and network traffic to identify potential threats early. Mobile intrusion detection protects devices by alerting users or blocking harmful actions before significant damage occurs. It uses techniques such as signature-based detection and machine learning algorithms to recognize known and emerging attacks. Challenges include resource constraints on mobile devices and adapting to evolving threats. By providing real-time monitoring and alerts, mobile intrusion detection significantly enhances security in mobile computing environments.

82. How does mobile computing support e-governance services?
Answer: Mobile computing supports e-governance services by enabling citizens to access government resources, submit documents, pay bills, and receive notifications using their mobile devices. Mobile apps and SMS services allow efficient delivery of public services like healthcare appointments, tax filing, and voting information. This accessibility improves transparency, reduces administrative costs, and bridges the gap between governments and citizens, especially in remote areas. Challenges include ensuring data privacy, building user-friendly interfaces, and providing multi-language support. Despite these hurdles, mobile computing strengthens governance by improving public service efficiency and fostering active citizen participation in administrative processes.

83. What is the difference between native apps and hybrid apps in mobile computing?
Answer: Native apps are developed specifically for a particular operating system, such as Android or iOS, using platform-specific languages like Java or Swift. They offer high performance, access to device features, and seamless user experiences but require separate development for each platform. Hybrid apps, on the other hand, are built using web technologies like HTML, CSS, and JavaScript, then wrapped in a native container to run on multiple platforms. Hybrid apps are cost-effective and faster to develop but may offer reduced performance compared to native apps. The choice depends on project requirements, budget, and desired user experience in mobile computing.

84. Explain the role of mobile payment gateways in digital transactions.
Answer: Mobile payment gateways are secure platforms that facilitate digital transactions by processing payments between users and merchants through mobile devices. They encrypt sensitive information, verify credentials, and ensure funds are transferred safely. Examples include PayPal, Stripe, and Razorpay. Mobile payment gateways simplify online shopping, in-app purchases, and contactless payments, driving the growth of mobile commerce. They support multiple payment methods, including credit cards, mobile wallets, and UPI. Challenges include ensuring robust security, minimizing transaction failures, and complying with financial regulations. By offering seamless, secure payment solutions, these gateways are pivotal to the convenience and success of mobile transactions.

85. What is mobile responsive design, and why is it essential for websites?
Answer: Mobile responsive design ensures that websites automatically adapt their layout, content, and functionality to fit various screen sizes and orientations of mobile devices. It enhances usability by eliminating the need for zooming or horizontal scrolling, providing a consistent and optimized experience across devices. Responsive design is essential because a large proportion of users access websites via smartphones and tablets. It improves search engine rankings, user engagement, and accessibility. Challenges include designing for diverse devices and maintaining performance. Implementing responsive design is critical for businesses to reach wider audiences and deliver effective user experiences in mobile-driven digital environments.

86. How does mobile computing support environmental monitoring?
Answer: Mobile computing supports environmental monitoring by enabling data collection, analysis, and visualization through mobile devices and connected sensors. Mobile applications gather real-time information on air quality, water levels, noise pollution, and weather conditions, providing actionable insights for researchers and policymakers. Citizens also contribute data through crowdsourcing apps, enhancing coverage and accuracy. Mobile computing improves responsiveness during environmental crises like floods or wildfires by enabling timely alerts and resource coordination. Challenges include ensuring data accuracy, device compatibility, and network coverage in remote areas. Despite these, mobile computing empowers proactive environmental management and raises public awareness about sustainability issues.

87. What is mobile multi-tasking, and how is it achieved?
Answer: Mobile multi-tasking allows users to run multiple applications simultaneously on their devices, improving efficiency and convenience. It is achieved through operating system features like background processing, split-screen modes, and app switching mechanisms. For example, users can stream music while browsing the web or respond to messages while video calling. Mobile multi-tasking is essential for productivity and enhances user experience by minimizing interruptions. Challenges include managing battery life, memory allocation, and preventing system slowdowns. Effective multi-tasking requires optimized software and hardware to ensure smooth performance, allowing mobile devices to handle various tasks seamlessly without affecting functionality or speed.

88. Explain the concept of mobile caching and its benefits.
Answer: Mobile caching involves storing frequently accessed data locally on a mobile device to reduce network requests, improve application performance, and enhance user experience. Caching benefits users by enabling faster content loading, reducing bandwidth usage, and allowing limited offline access to applications. For example, video streaming apps use caching to preload portions of videos for smoother playback. Developers implement caching strategies such as memory caching, disk caching, or content delivery networks (CDNs) to balance performance and storage. Challenges include managing cache size, ensuring data consistency, and protecting cached sensitive information. Proper caching significantly improves mobile application efficiency and responsiveness.

89. What is the significance of mobile API integration?
Answer: Mobile API (Application Programming Interface) integration enables mobile applications to interact with external services, platforms, or devices, providing enhanced functionalities without building features from scratch. APIs allow apps to access maps, payment gateways, social media platforms, or cloud storage seamlessly. They simplify development, promote interoperability, and reduce costs. For instance, integrating Google Maps API enables location services within a mobile app. Challenges include managing API security, version compatibility, and dependency risks. Mobile API integration is vital for creating feature-rich applications, ensuring faster development cycles, and delivering seamless user experiences in today's interconnected mobile computing landscape.

90. How does mobile computing aid in healthcare delivery systems?
Answer: Mobile computing aids healthcare delivery systems by enabling remote consultations, electronic health record access, patient monitoring, and appointment scheduling via smartphones and tablets. Mobile apps allow patients to book visits, receive medication reminders, and track health metrics. For healthcare providers, mobile computing supports quick decision-making, telemedicine services, and improved collaboration among teams. It also enhances healthcare accessibility in rural areas. Challenges include ensuring patient data privacy, regulatory compliance, and device security. Despite these issues, mobile computing transforms healthcare by improving efficiency, reducing operational costs, and delivering personalized care, leading to better patient outcomes and overall system effectiveness.

91. What is mobile edge analytics, and why is it important?
Answer: Mobile edge analytics refers to analyzing data directly at the network edge, close to where it is generated, rather than sending it to a centralized cloud server. This approach reduces latency, conserves bandwidth, and supports real-time decision-making, crucial for mobile applications like autonomous vehicles, augmented reality, and IoT devices. Mobile edge analytics enables faster insights, enhances privacy by keeping sensitive data local, and improves the efficiency of resource-constrained mobile environments. Challenges include limited processing power at the edge and managing distributed analytics workloads. Despite these, it plays a vital role in enabling intelligent, responsive, and resource-efficient mobile computing systems.

92. How does mobile computing enable location-based advertising?
Answer: Mobile computing enables location-based advertising by leveraging GPS, Wi-Fi, and Bluetooth to deliver personalized promotions to users based on their current location. For example, a retail app can send a discount notification when a user is near a store. This approach increases marketing effectiveness by targeting users at the right place and time. It benefits businesses through higher conversion rates and improved customer engagement. However, challenges include user privacy concerns, battery drain, and the need for accurate location data. When implemented ethically, location-based advertising enhances user experiences and creates opportunities for businesses to connect meaningfully with customers.

93. What is mobile sensor fusion, and how does it work?
Answer: Mobile sensor fusion combines data from multiple sensors on a mobile device to improve accuracy, reliability, and performance in applications. For example, integrating GPS, accelerometers, and gyroscopes enhances navigation systems by compensating for signal loss in urban areas. Sensor fusion enables advanced features like gesture recognition, indoor positioning, and augmented reality. It improves user experiences by delivering more precise information and reducing errors. Challenges include processing complexity, sensor calibration, and energy efficiency. Despite these challenges, sensor fusion has become a key enabler of sophisticated mobile applications, helping devices adapt intelligently to dynamic environments and user interactions.

94. Explain how mobile computing supports remote workforce management.
Answer: Mobile computing supports remote workforce management by enabling employees to access corporate systems, communicate with teams, and perform tasks from any location using mobile devices. Applications like Slack, Zoom, and project management tools allow seamless collaboration, time tracking, and task updates in real-time. Mobile computing increases flexibility, enhances productivity, and supports hybrid work models. Challenges include maintaining data security, managing device diversity, and ensuring reliable connectivity. Organizations often implement mobile device management (MDM) solutions to mitigate risks. By empowering remote employees, mobile computing helps companies remain agile, reduce overhead costs, and retain talent in today's evolving workplace environments.

95. What is mobile deep learning, and what are its applications?
Answer: Mobile deep learning brings artificial intelligence capabilities to mobile devices by deploying neural network models directly on smartphones and tablets. It enables applications such as facial recognition, voice assistants, real-time language translation, and predictive text input without relying entirely on cloud processing. Mobile deep learning enhances privacy by processing data locally and reduces latency for critical tasks. Challenges include computational limitations, battery consumption, and model optimization for resource-constrained environments. Despite these, mobile deep learning empowers developers to create intelligent, context-aware applications, transforming how users interact with their devices and enabling advanced functionalities in mobile computing ecosystems.

96. How does mobile computing support disaster recovery systems?
Answer: Mobile computing supports disaster recovery systems by enabling rapid communication, resource coordination, and data access during emergencies. Mobile devices allow authorities to send alerts, manage rescue operations, and monitor affected areas using GPS and mobile networks. Mobile apps help volunteers coordinate efforts and provide real-time updates to responders. Cloud-based mobile solutions ensure critical data is backed up and accessible even if local infrastructure is damaged. Challenges include ensuring network availability in disaster zones and protecting sensitive information. Mobile computing enhances resilience, speeds response times, and ensures continuity of operations, making it an essential component of modern disaster recovery strategies.

97. What is mobile virtualization, and how does it enhance security?
Answer: Mobile virtualization allows multiple operating systems or isolated environments to run on a single mobile device. It creates separate workspaces, ensuring that corporate data is isolated from personal applications, thus enhancing security in Bring Your Own Device (BYOD) scenarios. Virtualization prevents malware in personal apps from accessing sensitive corporate information. It also simplifies device management for IT teams by allowing remote updates and monitoring of virtual environments. Challenges include performance overhead and limited hardware resources on mobile devices. Despite these, mobile virtualization is a valuable tool for improving security, compliance, and operational efficiency in enterprise mobile computing environments.

98. Explain the significance of mobile predictive analytics.
Answer: Mobile predictive analytics uses historical data, machine learning, and algorithms to anticipate user behavior and trends on mobile devices. It enables personalized recommendations, targeted advertising, and proactive system optimizations like battery management or network usage predictions. Businesses use predictive analytics in mobile apps to enhance customer engagement, forecast demands, and reduce churn rates. Challenges include ensuring data privacy, managing computational requirements, and avoiding biases in predictions. Proper implementation of predictive analytics improves user experiences, boosts operational efficiency, and helps companies make data-driven decisions, making it an increasingly critical component in mobile computing and digital business strategies.

99. What is mobile edge computing, and how does it reduce latency?
Answer: Mobile edge computing (MEC) processes data closer to the user's device at the network edge instead of relying on distant cloud servers. By reducing the physical distance data travels, MEC minimizes latency, enabling real-time applications like autonomous driving, video conferencing, and augmented reality. MEC also reduces network congestion and improves privacy by processing sensitive information locally. Challenges include infrastructure deployment, resource allocation, and integrating MEC with existing mobile networks. Despite these, MEC plays a vital role in delivering ultra-fast, low-latency mobile experiences and supports the scalability of next-generation mobile applications in IoT and 5G ecosystems.

100. How does mobile computing enhance user personalization in applications?
Answer: Mobile computing enhances user personalization by leveraging device sensors, user behavior data, and context-aware technologies to tailor application content and experiences. Applications can adapt based on user location, preferences, and usage history to deliver relevant recommendations, targeted notifications, and customized interfaces. Personalization improves user engagement, satisfaction, and loyalty by making applications feel more intuitive and responsive to individual needs. Challenges include maintaining data privacy, preventing over-personalization fatigue, and balancing customization with usability. When implemented effectively, personalization transforms mobile applications into highly adaptive tools that align closely with user expectations and lifestyles, driving the success of mobile computing platforms.

101. What is the role of mobile computing in supply chain management?
Answer: Mobile computing plays a crucial role in supply chain management by enabling real-time tracking of goods, inventory updates, and seamless communication between stakeholders. Mobile devices allow employees to scan barcodes, monitor shipments, and access critical data from anywhere. GPS integration supports route optimization and reduces delivery times. Cloud-based mobile applications improve collaboration between suppliers, warehouses, and distributors. Challenges include network reliability, data security, and device compatibility across supply chain systems. Despite these, mobile computing enhances efficiency, visibility, and decision-making in supply chains, ensuring faster responses to market demands and improving overall operational effectiveness for businesses globally.

102. How does mobile computing support smart agriculture?
Answer: Mobile computing supports smart agriculture by empowering farmers with real-time access to weather forecasts, crop health data, and precision farming tools. Mobile apps enable soil analysis, irrigation scheduling, and pest monitoring, improving agricultural productivity and sustainability. Sensors integrated with mobile devices track environmental conditions, providing actionable insights to farmers. GPS and drones enhance land mapping and resource management. Challenges include rural network connectivity and the need for user-friendly interfaces. By bridging the digital divide, mobile computing revolutionizes agriculture, allowing farmers to make data-driven decisions that increase crop yields, reduce waste, and ensure sustainable food production worldwide.

103. Explain how mobile computing enables digital wallets.
Answer: Mobile computing enables digital wallets by transforming smartphones into secure platforms for storing payment information and conducting financial transactions. Users can link bank accounts, credit cards, or cryptocurrencies to apps like Google Pay, Apple Wallet, or Paytm for contactless payments. Digital wallets leverage NFC, QR codes, and biometric authentication for secure, convenient transactions in physical stores and online shopping. They also support bill payments, ticket bookings, and peer-to-peer transfers. Challenges include ensuring data encryption, protecting user privacy, and preventing fraud. Despite these concerns, digital wallets offer convenience and have become integral to mobile commerce in today's cashless economy.

104. What is mobile app sandboxing, and why is it important?
Answer: Mobile app sandboxing isolates applications in secure environments to prevent them from accessing unauthorized data or interfering with other apps on a device. This security mechanism restricts an app's access to system resources, reducing risks from malware or compromised software. Sandboxing is crucial in mobile computing because users frequently download third-party apps that could carry hidden vulnerabilities. It protects sensitive information like passwords, contacts, and banking details from being exposed. Challenges include balancing security with app functionality and performance. Sandboxing strengthens mobile security, ensuring apps operate safely without compromising the integrity of the overall system or other applications.

105. How does mobile computing enable telehealth services?
Answer: Mobile computing enables telehealth services by allowing patients and healthcare providers to connect remotely through smartphones, tablets, and health monitoring apps. Video consultations, electronic prescriptions, and real-time health data sharing make healthcare accessible to people in remote or underserved areas. Mobile devices integrate with wearable sensors to monitor vitals like heart rate and glucose levels, sending data to doctors instantly. Challenges include ensuring secure data transmission, addressing privacy concerns, and managing network limitations in rural regions. Despite these issues, telehealth powered by mobile computing improves healthcare accessibility, reduces hospital visits, and supports proactive, patient-centered medical care.

106. What is mobile data offloading, and how does it improve network efficiency?
Answer: Mobile data offloading refers to diverting traffic from congested cellular networks to alternative networks like Wi-Fi or small cells to improve performance and reduce load on mobile infrastructure. Offloading enhances user experience by offering faster data speeds and minimizes strain on mobile service providers during peak usage times. It is critical for handling increasing mobile data demands, especially in urban areas. Challenges include ensuring seamless transitions between networks, security over public Wi-Fi, and user consent. Mobile data offloading improves network efficiency, lowers operational costs, and supports consistent connectivity in mobile computing ecosystems.

107. Explain the significance of mobile analytics in improving business strategies.
Answer: Mobile analytics collects and analyzes user interaction data from mobile applications to provide insights into user behavior, preferences, and engagement patterns. Businesses leverage mobile analytics to improve app design, personalize marketing campaigns, and enhance customer experiences. Key metrics include session duration, retention rates, and conversion funnels. Real-time analytics supports decision-making and optimization strategies to drive growth. Challenges involve maintaining user privacy, managing large datasets, and ensuring compliance with regulations like GDPR. Despite these hurdles, mobile analytics empowers businesses to align their strategies with user needs, increase customer loyalty, and achieve competitive advantages in mobile-driven markets.

108. What is mobile app containerization, and how does it enhance security?
Answer: Mobile app containerization involves isolating enterprise applications and their data in a secure, encrypted container within a mobile device. This approach separates corporate data from personal apps and files, preventing unauthorized access and data leakage. Containerization is critical in Bring Your Own Device (BYOD) environments, where employees use personal devices for work. IT administrators can enforce security policies, remotely wipe corporate data if needed, and manage apps without interfering with personal content. Challenges include potential performance impacts and ensuring user adoption. Mobile app containerization strengthens enterprise security while supporting flexibility and productivity in mobile computing environments.

109. Describe the impact of wearable devices on mobile computing.
Answer: Wearable devices like smartwatches, fitness bands, and AR glasses have expanded mobile computing by

providing continuous monitoring, real-time notifications, and hands-free interactions. They integrate with smartphones to deliver health insights, location tracking, and quick access to applications. Wearables support industries like healthcare, fitness, and logistics by enabling on-the-go data collection and communication. Challenges include limited battery life, data privacy concerns, and ensuring compatibility across platforms. Despite these issues, wearables enrich user experiences, promote wellness, and enhance productivity, making them an essential extension of mobile computing ecosystems and driving innovations in personal and professional applications.

110. How does mobile computing contribute to autonomous vehicles?
Answer: Mobile computing contributes to autonomous vehicles by enabling real-time data processing, communication, and navigation through advanced mobile networks and edge computing. Mobile devices support vehicle-to-everything (V2X) communication, allowing cars to exchange information with traffic systems, pedestrians, and other vehicles. Mobile computing enables remote diagnostics, software updates, and driver assistance features like lane detection and collision avoidance. Challenges include ensuring ultra-low latency, data security, and robust connectivity in varying environments. Despite these hurdles, mobile computing serves as the backbone for autonomous vehicle ecosystems, facilitating safer, more efficient, and smarter transportation systems globally.

111. What is mobile content delivery optimization, and why is it important?
Answer: Mobile content delivery optimization involves enhancing the way digital content is delivered to mobile devices to ensure faster loading times, reduced data usage, and improved user experiences. Techniques include compressing media files, caching content closer to users through Content Delivery Networks (CDNs), and adapting content for various screen sizes and bandwidth conditions. It is essential because mobile users often experience variable network speeds and device constraints. Challenges include maintaining content quality, managing dynamic user requests, and ensuring compatibility across devices. Proper optimization ensures efficient resource utilization and keeps users engaged by providing smooth, responsive mobile application and browsing experiences.

112. How does mobile computing enable location-based emergency services?
Answer: Mobile computing enables location-based emergency services by using GPS, cell tower triangulation, and Wi-Fi positioning to pinpoint a user's location during emergencies. Services like eCall in vehicles and mobile 112 systems can automatically transmit a user's coordinates to first responders for faster assistance. Mobile apps also send real-time alerts about nearby hazards or natural disasters. Challenges include ensuring location accuracy in remote areas and protecting sensitive user data. By integrating mobile technologies, emergency services become more responsive, efficient, and life-saving, improving public safety and allowing authorities to deploy resources effectively during critical situations.

113. What is mobile augmented reality navigation, and how does it work?
Answer: Mobile augmented reality (AR) navigation overlays digital information like directional arrows, street names, and landmarks onto a user's real-world environment using a smartphone camera or AR glasses. It enhances traditional GPS by providing a more intuitive, immersive navigation experience. Applications like Google Maps' AR mode guide users through unfamiliar areas with real-time visual cues. Challenges include ensuring accuracy in dense urban areas, battery consumption, and requiring high-performance devices. Despite these hurdles, AR navigation simplifies wayfinding, especially for pedestrians and tourists, offering a transformative approach to exploring cities and improving user confidence in navigating new environments.

114. Explain mobile computing's role in financial inclusion.
Answer: Mobile computing drives financial inclusion by providing access to banking and financial services through mobile devices, particularly for unbanked populations in remote or underserved regions. Mobile banking apps, digital wallets, and microfinance platforms enable users to make payments, transfer funds, and manage savings without physical bank branches. Services like M-Pesa in Africa illustrate mobile computing's power to empower marginalized communities economically. Challenges include ensuring security, improving digital literacy, and expanding reliable network coverage. By bridging the gap between financial institutions and users, mobile computing fosters economic participation, reduces inequality, and supports sustainable development worldwide.

115. What is mobile device geofencing, and how is it used in businesses?
Answer: Mobile device geofencing creates virtual boundaries around specific geographic areas and triggers predefined actions when a mobile device enters or exits these zones. Businesses use geofencing for marketing, security, and

operations. For example, retailers send promotional offers to customers near their stores, while enterprises track employee attendance at work sites. Geofencing also supports fleet management and location-based notifications. Challenges include battery drain from constant location tracking and user privacy concerns. When implemented responsibly, geofencing improves customer engagement, streamlines operations, and provides valuable location-based insights, making it a powerful tool in mobile computing for various industries.

116. How does mobile computing enhance customer service in businesses?
Answer: Mobile computing enhances customer service by enabling businesses to interact with customers instantly through mobile apps, chatbots, and real-time support platforms. Customers can submit queries, track orders, and provide feedback from anywhere. Businesses use mobile notifications to update users about services, appointments, or issues proactively. Challenges include managing response times, ensuring seamless app functionality, and safeguarding customer data. Mobile technologies empower customer service teams to access information remotely, resolve issues faster, and deliver personalized support, leading to higher customer satisfaction and loyalty. As mobile use grows, businesses increasingly rely on mobile computing to strengthen customer relationships.

117. What is mobile network slicing, and why is it important in 5G?
Answer: Mobile network slicing is a technique in 5G that divides a physical network into multiple virtual networks, each tailored to specific applications or services. For example, one slice can prioritize autonomous vehicles with ultra-low latency, while another supports streaming with high bandwidth. Network slicing is crucial because it enables efficient resource allocation, supports diverse use cases, and enhances service quality for mobile computing environments. Challenges include managing security across slices, orchestrating resources, and ensuring interoperability. This technology makes 5G highly adaptable, empowering mobile applications in industries like healthcare, IoT, and entertainment with optimized and reliable connectivity.

118. Explain the concept of mobile edge caching and its benefits.
Answer: Mobile edge caching stores frequently accessed data at the network edge, closer to users, to reduce latency and improve content delivery in mobile computing. It benefits users by enabling faster load times for apps, videos, and websites, particularly during peak network traffic. Businesses use edge caching to deliver smoother streaming experiences and minimize server load. Challenges include managing storage limits, ensuring data freshness, and protecting cached sensitive information. By reducing reliance on distant servers, mobile edge caching optimizes bandwidth usage, enhances performance, and improves user experiences, making it a key component in modern mobile networks and applications.

119. How does mobile computing support e-learning platforms?
Answer: Mobile computing supports e-learning platforms by enabling students and educators to access educational content, live classes, and collaborative tools from any location via smartphones and tablets. Mobile apps provide interactive lessons, quizzes, and notifications, enhancing learner engagement and flexibility. Features like offline content access and adaptive learning personalize education for diverse learners. Challenges include ensuring equitable access to devices and internet connectivity, maintaining learner focus, and securing student data. Mobile computing democratizes education, supporting continuous learning opportunities and making knowledge accessible globally, especially for individuals in remote areas or those with limited access to traditional educational infrastructure.

120. What is mobile proximity marketing, and how does it work?
Answer: Mobile proximity marketing delivers targeted messages, promotions, or content to users based on their physical proximity to a business or location using technologies like Bluetooth beacons, NFC, or Wi-Fi. Retailers use proximity marketing to engage nearby customers with personalized offers or product recommendations in real-time. It increases foot traffic, boosts sales, and enhances customer experiences through timely, relevant interactions. Challenges include user privacy concerns, permission management, and avoiding excessive notifications that may annoy customers. When implemented thoughtfully, mobile proximity marketing creates meaningful connections between businesses and customers, driving loyalty and engagement in highly competitive marketplaces.

121. Describe mobile application lifecycle management (MALM).
Answer: Mobile application lifecycle management (MALM) refers to the process of managing a mobile app from its initial development through deployment, updates, maintenance, and eventual retirement. MALM ensures that apps remain functional, secure, and relevant as user needs and technologies evolve. It involves stages like planning, testing,

release management, monitoring, and continuous improvement. Businesses use MALM to streamline workflows, ensure compliance, and minimize downtime. Challenges include adapting to rapid platform changes, ensuring backward compatibility, and managing user feedback efficiently. Effective MALM practices support robust, user-friendly mobile apps that meet organizational goals and deliver consistent value to end users.

122. How does mobile computing enable vehicle-to-everything (V2X) communication?
Answer: Mobile computing enables Vehicle-to-Everything (V2X) communication by allowing vehicles to exchange information with other vehicles, infrastructure, pedestrians, and networks in real-time. V2X enhances road safety, reduces traffic congestion, and supports autonomous driving through technologies like LTE, 5G, and dedicated short-range communications (DSRC). Vehicles receive alerts about hazards, signal changes, or nearby pedestrians, enabling proactive responses. Challenges include ensuring ultra-low latency, interoperability between systems, and data security. Mobile computing provides the backbone for V2X systems, transforming transportation into a connected ecosystem that improves efficiency, safety, and environmental sustainability for modern mobility solutions.

123. What is mobile biometrics, and how is it used in authentication?
Answer: Mobile biometrics uses unique biological traits such as fingerprints, facial recognition, voice patterns, or iris scans to verify user identity on mobile devices. It replaces traditional passwords, offering faster, more secure authentication for unlocking devices, authorizing transactions, and accessing applications. Biometric systems rely on sensors integrated into smartphones and tablets to capture and process biometric data. Challenges include spoofing attempts, sensor accuracy limitations, and protecting biometric data from breaches. Despite these, mobile biometrics has become a cornerstone of mobile security, balancing convenience and protection, and enhancing user confidence in handling sensitive personal and financial information on their devices.

124. Explain mobile app performance optimization techniques.
Answer: Mobile app performance optimization involves improving app speed, responsiveness, and stability to enhance user experiences. Techniques include minimizing network requests, compressing media files, reducing memory usage, and leveraging efficient coding practices. Developers use tools like profiling and analytics to identify bottlenecks and optimize UI rendering for smoother interactions. Caching strategies and asynchronous processing also play critical roles in improving performance. Challenges include balancing optimization with feature-rich functionality and ensuring consistent performance across diverse devices. Proper optimization ensures user retention, positive app reviews, and higher engagement, making it essential in the competitive landscape of mobile computing applications.

125. What is mobile computing's role in the sharing economy?
Answer: Mobile computing drives the sharing economy by connecting service providers and consumers through mobile platforms, enabling peer-to-peer transactions. Apps like Uber, Airbnb, and TaskRabbit rely on mobile computing to facilitate booking, payments, and real-time communication between users. Mobile devices provide GPS tracking, instant notifications, and secure payment processing, creating seamless user experiences. Challenges include managing regulatory compliance, ensuring data privacy, and maintaining trust among users. Despite these, mobile computing has revolutionized industries by enabling flexible, convenient, and cost-effective access to shared resources, fostering innovation and empowering individuals to participate in new economic models globally.

Chapter 5: Most Asked Questions Part-B

1. What is the difference between mobile computing and traditional computing?

Answer: Mobile computing enables users to access data, applications, and communication services from portable devices without being confined to a specific location. In contrast, traditional computing relies on stationary desktop systems with fixed network connections. Mobile computing offers flexibility, real-time access, and on-the-go productivity, making it essential in today's fast-paced world. However, it faces challenges like battery constraints and variable network connectivity. Traditional computing provides higher processing power and storage but lacks mobility. Together, both paradigms support diverse user needs, with mobile computing increasingly dominating personal and professional workflows in modern digital ecosystems.

2. Explain mobile device management (MDM) and its importance in enterprises.

Answer: Mobile Device Management (MDM) is a security solution enabling IT teams to monitor, secure, and manage employee mobile devices in corporate environments. It ensures that devices comply with security policies, manages app installations, and allows remote data wiping in case of theft or loss. MDM is crucial for enterprises adopting Bring Your Own Device (BYOD) policies to protect sensitive corporate data across a diverse range of mobile platforms. Challenges include maintaining user privacy and supporting multiple operating systems. Effective MDM enhances productivity and security by providing centralized control over enterprise mobile infrastructures.

3. How does mobile computing contribute to e-commerce growth?

Answer: Mobile computing drives e-commerce growth by enabling users to shop online from anywhere through smartphones and tablets. Mobile apps and responsive websites provide personalized recommendations, seamless payment systems, and real-time customer support. Push notifications keep users engaged with promotions and order updates. Challenges include ensuring app security, optimizing performance for diverse devices, and managing digital payment risks. Despite these, mobile computing transforms e-commerce by offering convenience, expanding market reach, and enabling innovative shopping experiences like AR-powered virtual try-ons. Businesses leveraging mobile platforms gain competitive advantages in the rapidly evolving retail landscape.

4. What is mobile peer-to-peer (P2P) communication, and how is it used?

Answer: Mobile peer-to-peer (P2P) communication allows devices to connect directly without centralized servers, enabling file sharing, collaborative applications, and local networking. Technologies such as Wi-Fi Direct and Bluetooth power P2P mobile interactions. Applications include offline file transfers, multiplayer gaming, and content sharing in remote areas where internet connectivity is limited. Challenges involve security risks, limited range, and bandwidth constraints. Despite these limitations, mobile P2P enhances flexibility, reduces dependency on traditional infrastructure, and supports innovative services in both personal and professional mobile computing scenarios.

5. Describe the concept of mobile cloud computing and its benefits.

Answer: Mobile Cloud Computing (MCC) integrates mobile devices with cloud-based services to overcome hardware and software limitations. MCC enables applications to offload processing and storage tasks to remote servers, allowing lightweight devices to run resource-intensive apps. Benefits include enhanced scalability, extended battery life, and access to data across devices. Examples include cloud storage apps like Google Drive and productivity tools like Office 365. Challenges include ensuring reliable connectivity, data security, and latency management. MCC empowers users with powerful, flexible mobile experiences, bridging the gap between limited device capabilities and demanding application requirements.

6. What are mobile computing's main components?

Answer: Mobile computing comprises three main components: mobile hardware, mobile software, and wireless communication networks. Mobile hardware includes devices such as smartphones, tablets, and wearables that allow users to access applications and services on the go. Mobile software consists of operating systems and applications optimized for portability and limited resources. Wireless communication networks like Wi-Fi, LTE, and 5G provide seamless connectivity for data transfer and communication. Together, these components enable mobility, real-time access, and enhanced user experiences in diverse personal, professional, and industrial environments.

7. Explain the role of mobile sensors in healthcare applications.
Answer: Mobile sensors integrated into smartphones and wearables monitor health metrics such as heart rate, sleep patterns, and physical activity. In healthcare applications, these sensors provide real-time data to physicians for diagnosis, treatment adjustments, and remote patient monitoring. For example, glucose monitors paired with mobile apps help diabetics manage their condition more effectively. Challenges include ensuring sensor accuracy, maintaining data privacy, and integrating with existing healthcare systems. Despite these issues, mobile sensors enhance preventive care, reduce hospital visits, and empower patients to take charge of their health through accessible, user-friendly solutions.

8. What is mobile application virtualization, and how does it work?
Answer: Mobile application virtualization allows apps to run in isolated environments separate from the device's core operating system. It enables enterprises to deploy corporate applications securely without directly installing them on user devices. Virtualization ensures data stays within a controlled sandbox, enhancing security and simplifying management. Employees can access apps from any device without risking data leakage into personal spaces. Challenges include potential performance trade-offs and network dependency. Mobile app virtualization is an essential tool for enterprises adopting BYOD strategies, ensuring flexibility while maintaining stringent security standards across diverse mobile ecosystems.

9. How does mobile computing improve disaster response systems?
Answer: Mobile computing enhances disaster response by enabling real-time communication, GPS tracking, and coordination among rescue teams. Mobile apps provide instant alerts to citizens, guide them to safe zones, and facilitate volunteer mobilization. Drone integration with mobile networks supports rapid damage assessment and resource allocation. Challenges include ensuring network availability during disasters and protecting sensitive data. Mobile computing provides resilience and agility in emergency scenarios, improving response times, reducing casualties, and supporting data-driven decision-making in life-critical situations.

10. What is the significance of mobile-based digital identity solutions?
Answer: Mobile-based digital identity solutions use smartphones to verify user identities securely in online and offline transactions. Techniques include biometric authentication, one-time passwords (OTPs), and encrypted digital IDs stored on devices. These solutions are crucial for accessing banking services, government portals, and e-commerce platforms without physical documents. Benefits include convenience, reduced fraud risks, and enhanced accessibility for remote populations. Challenges involve safeguarding personal data and ensuring compatibility across diverse platforms. Mobile digital identities are transforming how users prove their identity, making interactions seamless and secure in mobile computing environments.

11. How does mobile computing support Internet of Things (IoT) applications?
Answer: Mobile computing supports IoT applications by enabling real-time communication and control of connected devices through smartphones and tablets. Mobile apps act as user interfaces for managing IoT ecosystems, from smart homes to industrial systems. For instance, users can adjust thermostats, monitor security cameras, or track fitness data remotely. Mobile devices leverage wireless technologies like Bluetooth, Wi-Fi, and 5G to communicate with IoT sensors and actuators. Challenges include data security, battery constraints, and ensuring interoperability between devices. Despite these, mobile computing enhances IoT accessibility, empowering users with seamless, on-the-go control over diverse connected devices in personal and professional contexts.

12. What is mobile edge computing, and why is it essential in modern networks?
Answer: Mobile edge computing (MEC) processes data closer to users at the network edge rather than relying solely on centralized cloud servers. This approach reduces latency, improves bandwidth efficiency, and supports real-time applications like autonomous vehicles and augmented reality. MEC is essential in modern networks to meet the growing demand for high-speed, low-latency services in mobile computing. Challenges include deploying infrastructure, managing distributed resources, and ensuring robust security. MEC enables faster response times and enhanced user experiences, making it a critical component in 5G and IoT ecosystems where split-second decisions and efficient data handling are vital.

13. Explain the role of mobile computing in environmental sustainability.
Answer: Mobile computing contributes to environmental sustainability by reducing paper usage through digital

communications, enabling smart energy management systems, and supporting eco-friendly transportation solutions like ride-sharing apps. Mobile applications track carbon footprints, promote sustainable practices, and facilitate recycling programs. IoT sensors connected to mobile networks monitor air quality, water usage, and waste levels for more efficient resource management. Challenges include e-waste from mobile devices and energy consumption of mobile networks. Despite this, mobile computing plays a positive role in promoting awareness and providing tools for individuals and organizations to adopt environmentally responsible behaviors and reduce their ecological impact.

14. What is mobile virtual network operator (MVNO), and how does it function?
Answer: A Mobile Virtual Network Operator (MVNO) is a wireless service provider that does not own network infrastructure but leases it from major carriers to offer services under its brand. MVNOs purchase bulk access to network resources and provide customized plans targeting specific customer segments, often at competitive prices. They function by utilizing the parent network's towers and infrastructure while managing billing, customer service, and marketing independently. Challenges include limited control over network quality and dependency on agreements with major carriers. MVNOs enhance mobile service accessibility and competition, offering flexible options for users in diverse markets.

15. How do mobile computing systems handle real-time data processing?
Answer: Mobile computing systems handle real-time data processing through edge computing, efficient algorithms, and high-speed networks like 5G. Applications such as navigation, stock trading, and video conferencing rely on immediate data analysis and response. Techniques like caching, predictive analytics, and distributed computing help reduce latency and ensure timely results. Challenges include network interruptions, processing constraints on mobile devices, and balancing speed with accuracy. Despite these challenges, advancements in mobile processors and optimized software enable real-time capabilities, allowing mobile applications to provide instant feedback and seamless experiences crucial for time-sensitive user interactions.

16. What is mobile cloud storage, and what are its benefits?
Answer: Mobile cloud storage allows users to save data on remote servers accessed via mobile devices, rather than relying solely on local storage. Services like Google Drive, Dropbox, and iCloud enable users to store, retrieve, and share files anytime, anywhere. Benefits include freeing up device memory, facilitating collaboration, and ensuring data backup in case of device failure. Cloud storage supports synchronization across multiple devices for seamless workflows. Challenges involve ensuring data security, managing bandwidth usage, and complying with privacy regulations. Despite these concerns, mobile cloud storage enhances flexibility, productivity, and data accessibility for both personal and professional users.

17. Explain the concept of mobile application containerization.
Answer: Mobile application containerization isolates corporate applications and data within secure, encrypted containers on a mobile device. This ensures that enterprise information remains separate from personal apps and prevents data leakage. It is especially useful in Bring Your Own Device (BYOD) environments, allowing employees to use their devices for work without compromising security. IT teams can enforce policies, control access, and wipe corporate data if needed without affecting personal content. Challenges include user resistance and potential performance trade-offs. Mobile containerization strengthens enterprise security while maintaining flexibility for employees, supporting secure mobile computing in corporate environments.

18. How does mobile computing enable location-based services (LBS)?
Answer: Mobile computing enables location-based services (LBS) by using GPS, Wi-Fi positioning, and cell tower triangulation to determine a user's location. LBS provides personalized services like navigation, weather updates, restaurant suggestions, and location-targeted advertising. Businesses use LBS for customer engagement through geofencing and proximity marketing. Challenges include maintaining location accuracy, managing battery drain, and addressing user privacy concerns. Despite these, LBS enhances user experiences by delivering contextually relevant information and services, making mobile applications more interactive, personalized, and indispensable in daily life and professional workflows.

19. What are the challenges of mobile network handoff in mobile computing?
Answer: Mobile network handoff occurs when a user's device transitions between cell towers while maintaining an active connection. Challenges include ensuring seamless data transmission, minimizing dropped calls, and managing

latency during the switch. In fast-moving scenarios like driving, frequent handoffs may lead to signal degradation or temporary disconnections. Interference and resource allocation issues complicate smooth handoff processes. Advanced techniques such as soft handoff and predictive algorithms help mitigate these problems. Efficient handoff is critical for uninterrupted services in applications like video calls, streaming, and real-time navigation in mobile computing environments.

20. Describe mobile computing's role in enhancing accessibility for people with disabilities.
Answer: Mobile computing enhances accessibility by providing tools and features that empower people with disabilities to interact with technology. Screen readers, voice commands, haptic feedback, and text-to-speech functions support users with visual, auditory, or motor impairments. Applications allow for real-time translation of speech to text or vice versa, facilitating communication. Challenges include ensuring app compatibility with accessibility standards and addressing affordability barriers. Despite this, mobile devices have transformed the lives of individuals with disabilities, enabling independence, improving social participation, and granting access to essential services like healthcare, education, and employment opportunities.

21. What is mobile application scalability, and why is it important?
Answer: Mobile application scalability refers to an app's ability to handle increased user demand, data traffic, and feature growth without compromising performance. Scalable apps maintain speed, reliability, and responsiveness as user bases expand. Techniques to ensure scalability include using cloud backends, load balancing, and modular code design. Challenges involve predicting demand, managing costs, and ensuring consistent experiences across devices. Scalability is critical in mobile computing as applications like social media, e-commerce platforms, and streaming services often experience rapid user growth. Well-scaled mobile apps ensure long-term success and high user satisfaction in competitive markets.

22. How does mobile computing support smart healthcare systems?
Answer: Mobile computing supports smart healthcare systems by enabling real-time monitoring, telemedicine, and health data management through mobile devices and wearables. Patients use apps to schedule appointments, access medical records, and receive medication reminders. Doctors monitor patient vitals remotely and communicate through secure mobile platforms. Challenges include protecting patient privacy, ensuring device interoperability, and managing network reliability. Despite these, mobile computing increases healthcare accessibility, reduces costs, and improves patient outcomes. It empowers patients to manage their health proactively and supports healthcare professionals in delivering efficient, data-driven care.

23. What is mobile network virtualization, and how does it improve flexibility?
Answer: Mobile network virtualization abstracts physical network resources into multiple virtual networks, allowing efficient allocation and management of mobile services. It improves flexibility by enabling service providers to create customized networks for specific applications or user groups. For example, a virtual network can prioritize low-latency services for IoT devices while supporting high-bandwidth demands for video streaming. Challenges include managing security, ensuring compatibility, and orchestrating virtual resources efficiently. Mobile network virtualization supports cost savings, innovation, and scalability, making it an essential feature for 5G and next-generation mobile computing infrastructures.

24. Explain mobile artificial intelligence (AI) and its applications.
Answer: Mobile artificial intelligence (AI) integrates machine learning algorithms and neural networks into mobile devices, enabling smart functionalities without relying entirely on cloud processing. Applications include voice assistants, real-time language translation, predictive typing, and camera enhancements like facial recognition. AI enhances personalization and improves app efficiency by learning user behavior. Challenges involve optimizing AI models for limited device resources and ensuring data privacy. Mobile AI empowers devices to perform intelligent tasks on-device, reducing latency and improving responsiveness in mobile computing applications across industries such as healthcare, education, and e-commerce.

25. How does mobile computing enable ride-sharing platforms?
Answer: Mobile computing powers ride-sharing platforms like Uber and Lyft by connecting drivers and passengers through location-aware mobile applications. GPS tracks driver and rider locations in real time, while cloud servers process requests, calculate fares, and facilitate secure payments. Push notifications and in-app messaging enhance

communication and coordination. Challenges include ensuring app reliability during high-demand periods, safeguarding user data, and managing dynamic pricing algorithms. Mobile computing has revolutionized urban transportation, providing convenience, flexibility, and cost-effective mobility solutions while creating new economic opportunities in the gig economy.

26. What are mobile progressive web apps (PWAs), and how do they enhance user experiences?
Answer: Mobile progressive web apps (PWAs) combine the features of web and native apps to deliver fast, reliable, and engaging experiences directly through browsers. PWAs support offline functionality, push notifications, and home screen installation without needing an app store. They load quickly, adapt to different devices, and consume less storage than native apps. PWAs are valuable for businesses aiming to reach users across platforms efficiently. Challenges include limited access to device hardware and inconsistent browser support. Despite these, PWAs provide a seamless, cost-effective way to engage users, especially in areas with slow internet connections or limited device capabilities.

27. How does mobile computing support augmented reality (AR) applications?
Answer: Mobile computing supports augmented reality (AR) by enabling smartphones and tablets to overlay digital elements on the physical world through cameras and sensors. AR apps enhance gaming, education, retail, and navigation by providing interactive experiences. Examples include AR shopping apps that allow virtual product try-ons and AR games like Pokémon GO. Mobile devices use powerful processors, GPS, and motion sensors to deliver real-time AR content. Challenges include battery drain, processing demands, and ensuring accurate environment mapping. Despite these, mobile AR applications revolutionize how users interact with digital content, making mobile computing more immersive and engaging.

28. What is mobile device tethering, and what are its advantages?
Answer: Mobile device tethering allows a smartphone to share its cellular data connection with other devices like laptops and tablets, acting as a portable Wi-Fi hotspot. It is advantageous for accessing the internet in areas without Wi-Fi or during travel. Tethering enhances productivity by enabling remote work and seamless connectivity across devices. Challenges include increased battery consumption, high data usage, and potential restrictions from network providers. When used effectively, tethering transforms mobile devices into versatile tools for connectivity, offering users flexibility and convenience in managing their digital workflows from virtually anywhere.

29. Explain mobile digital marketing and its importance for businesses.
Answer: Mobile digital marketing leverages mobile platforms to promote products and services through channels like apps, SMS, push notifications, and social media. It allows businesses to target audiences with personalized campaigns based on user behavior and location. Mobile marketing increases customer engagement and drives sales by reaching users on devices they carry constantly. Techniques include in-app advertisements, mobile-friendly websites, and geofenced promotions. Challenges involve balancing frequency of notifications to avoid user fatigue and ensuring compliance with privacy regulations. Effective mobile marketing strategies are vital in today's digital economy, helping businesses remain competitive and build strong customer relationships.

30. How does mobile computing support real-time translation services?
Answer: Mobile computing enables real-time translation services by leveraging powerful processors, AI algorithms, and cloud connectivity on smartphones. Apps like Google Translate allow users to translate speech, text, or images instantly, breaking language barriers in travel, business, and education. Offline translation capabilities further enhance usability in areas with poor connectivity. Challenges include ensuring translation accuracy, supporting multiple languages, and managing privacy when processing sensitive content. Real-time mobile translation improves global communication, making mobile devices indispensable tools for cultural exchange and collaboration in personal and professional settings.

31. How does mobile computing enhance online learning for students?
Answer: Mobile computing enhances online learning by allowing students to access educational materials, attend virtual classes, and collaborate with peers anytime and anywhere through smartphones and tablets. Mobile apps provide interactive lessons, quizzes, and notifications that improve engagement. Features such as offline access enable learning even without internet connectivity, while cloud integration ensures seamless synchronization of notes and assignments across devices. Challenges include digital distractions, device compatibility, and ensuring equitable

access for all learners. Despite these, mobile computing promotes flexible, personalized learning experiences, empowering students to take control of their education in a digitally connected world.

32. What is mobile virtual reality (VR), and how is it applied?
Answer: Mobile virtual reality (VR) creates immersive 3D environments accessible through smartphones paired with VR headsets like Google Cardboard or Oculus Quest. Mobile VR is applied in gaming, education, healthcare, and real estate to provide realistic simulations and interactive experiences. For example, medical students use VR to practice surgical procedures, while travelers explore destinations virtually. Challenges include device performance limitations, motion sickness, and ensuring high-quality content. Despite these, mobile VR expands possibilities for interactive learning, entertainment, and professional training, making mobile computing a gateway to accessible and engaging virtual environments.

33. Explain the concept of mobile microtransactions in applications.
Answer: Mobile microtransactions involve small in-app purchases that allow users to buy digital goods or unlock premium features within mobile applications. Popular in gaming and subscription services, microtransactions generate revenue for developers while keeping app downloads free or low-cost. Examples include buying virtual currencies, skins, or ad-free experiences. Challenges include user concerns about overspending, ethical considerations in targeting young audiences, and ensuring secure payment processing. When implemented responsibly, microtransactions enhance user experiences and support sustainable business models in mobile computing, enabling developers to continuously innovate and maintain high-quality apps.

34. How does mobile computing enable smart retail solutions?
Answer: Mobile computing enables smart retail solutions by integrating smartphones, IoT devices, and cloud systems to enhance shopping experiences. Mobile apps allow customers to browse products, receive personalized offers, and make seamless digital payments. Retailers use mobile technologies for inventory management, real-time analytics, and contactless checkout systems. Location-based services like geofencing send targeted promotions to nearby shoppers. Challenges include securing customer data, ensuring app reliability, and balancing personalization with privacy concerns. Mobile computing transforms retail into an interactive, data-driven ecosystem that increases customer engagement, operational efficiency, and overall competitiveness in the market.

35. What is mobile wireless mesh networking, and where is it used?
Answer: Mobile wireless mesh networking connects multiple mobile devices directly to form a decentralized network where each device acts as a node, relaying data to others. It is used in disaster recovery, military operations, and rural areas with limited infrastructure to provide resilient, self-healing communication networks. Mesh networks support mobile computing by enabling connectivity without reliance on centralized access points. Challenges include managing interference, security risks, and ensuring efficient routing. Despite these, wireless mesh networks are valuable in scenarios requiring flexible, robust, and scalable connectivity solutions for mobile users in dynamic environments.

36. Explain the significance of mobile adaptive user interfaces.
Answer: Mobile adaptive user interfaces automatically adjust layouts, elements, and interactions based on device specifications, screen sizes, and user preferences. Adaptive interfaces ensure consistent, user-friendly experiences across diverse mobile devices, from smartphones to tablets. They accommodate varying resolutions, orientations, and accessibility needs, enhancing usability for all users, including those with disabilities. Challenges include maintaining performance, testing across devices, and balancing adaptability with design consistency. Effective adaptive interfaces are critical in mobile computing for delivering engaging, inclusive, and seamless experiences, increasing user satisfaction and app retention rates in competitive digital markets.

37. How does mobile computing support remote patient monitoring?
Answer: Mobile computing supports remote patient monitoring by enabling wearable devices and mobile apps to track vital signs such as heart rate, blood pressure, and glucose levels. Data collected from patients is transmitted securely to healthcare providers for real-time analysis and early intervention. This approach reduces hospital visits, supports chronic disease management, and improves healthcare accessibility in remote areas. Challenges include ensuring data privacy, managing network reliability, and integrating with existing healthcare systems. Mobile computing empowers

patients and healthcare professionals to collaborate effectively, enhancing treatment outcomes and reducing healthcare costs.

38. What is mobile crowdsourcing, and how is it applied?
Answer: Mobile crowdsourcing leverages the collective input of users on mobile devices to solve problems, gather data, or generate content. Applications include disaster response, traffic reporting (e.g., Waze), and product reviews. Mobile platforms distribute tasks to users and collect their contributions in real time, enabling large-scale collaboration. Challenges involve maintaining data quality, incentivizing participation, and addressing privacy concerns. Mobile crowdsourcing harnesses the power of connected communities, enabling businesses, governments, and organizations to access valuable insights and perform tasks that would otherwise require significant time and resources.

39. Explain the role of mobile computing in smart transportation systems.
Answer: Mobile computing plays a vital role in smart transportation by enabling real-time navigation, vehicle tracking, and traffic management through mobile apps and IoT sensors. Users access ride-hailing services, public transit updates, and parking solutions directly on their smartphones. Transportation authorities use mobile technologies to monitor road conditions and optimize traffic flow. Challenges include ensuring network reliability in high-density areas and addressing security concerns. Mobile computing improves urban mobility, reduces congestion, and enhances user convenience, making transportation systems more efficient, sustainable, and responsive to dynamic urban environments.

40. What are mobile push notifications, and how do they improve engagement?
Answer: Mobile push notifications are real-time alerts sent to users' devices, even when an app is not actively open. They inform users about updates, promotions, or reminders, keeping them engaged and encouraging them to return to the app. Push notifications are widely used in e-commerce, social media, and fitness apps to increase user retention and drive interactions. Challenges include preventing notification fatigue and managing user consent for receiving alerts. When implemented thoughtfully, push notifications enhance user experiences, strengthen brand loyalty, and ensure applications remain relevant in users' daily lives.

41. How does mobile computing assist in agricultural innovations?
Answer: Mobile computing assists agricultural innovations by providing farmers with tools for crop monitoring, weather forecasting, soil analysis, and pest detection via mobile apps. Smartphones and IoT sensors enable precision farming techniques, optimizing water and fertilizer usage while increasing crop yields. Mobile banking services facilitate access to microloans and insurance for farmers in rural areas. Challenges include ensuring digital literacy and reliable network coverage in remote locations. Mobile computing empowers agricultural communities with data-driven decision-making, improving productivity, sustainability, and food security in developing and developed nations alike.

42. What is mobile payment tokenization, and how does it secure transactions?
Answer: Mobile payment tokenization replaces sensitive payment details like credit card numbers with unique, encrypted tokens during transactions. This prevents hackers from accessing real account information if data is intercepted. Tokenization enhances security in mobile wallets and contactless payments by ensuring that actual card data is never stored on devices or transmitted over networks. Challenges include ensuring token management efficiency and integrating systems across different merchants and banks. Tokenization has become a cornerstone of secure mobile payments, increasing consumer trust and supporting the widespread adoption of digital payment technologies.

43. Explain mobile digital twins and their applications.
Answer: Mobile digital twins are virtual replicas of physical assets, systems, or processes that can be accessed and monitored through mobile devices. They are applied in industries like manufacturing, healthcare, and urban planning for real-time tracking, simulation, and predictive maintenance. Mobile access allows users to view, analyze, and interact with these digital models from anywhere, improving decision-making and operational efficiency. Challenges include ensuring real-time synchronization, managing large data volumes, and protecting sensitive information. Mobile digital twins enhance innovation and enable businesses to optimize operations proactively, reducing downtime and improving productivity.

44. How does mobile computing enable seamless remote work environments?
Answer: Mobile computing enables seamless remote work environments by providing employees with access to corporate tools, documents, and communication platforms through their mobile devices. Applications like Slack, Zoom, and cloud storage systems support collaboration and productivity from any location. Mobile VPNs ensure secure connections, while MDM solutions help IT teams manage devices effectively. Challenges include safeguarding sensitive data, ensuring reliable connectivity, and balancing work-life boundaries for employees. Mobile computing fosters flexible, agile workplaces, allowing organizations to maintain operations and employee engagement in an increasingly remote and distributed workforce.

45. What is mobile real-time data analytics, and why is it important?
Answer: Mobile real-time data analytics processes user behavior, transactions, and environmental data instantly to provide actionable insights. Businesses use this for personalized recommendations, fraud detection, and dynamic pricing strategies. Mobile apps in healthcare analyze patient vitals on the fly to trigger alerts for doctors. Challenges include managing large data streams, ensuring low-latency processing, and protecting user privacy. Real-time analytics is important because it enables rapid decision-making, enhances user experiences, and provides businesses with a competitive advantage in adapting to customer needs in dynamic mobile environments.

46. How does mobile computing support urban planning and smart cities?
Answer: Mobile computing supports urban planning and smart cities by integrating mobile apps, IoT devices, and data analytics to monitor traffic, air quality, and public services. Citizens use mobile apps to report issues, pay bills, or receive emergency notifications. Urban planners rely on mobile-generated data for better decision-making and resource allocation. Challenges include ensuring equitable access, managing infrastructure costs, and protecting user data. Mobile computing enhances efficiency, sustainability, and quality of life in urban environments, driving the development of intelligent, citizen-focused cities.

47. Explain the role of mobile computing in blockchain applications.
Answer: Mobile computing powers blockchain applications by enabling secure access to decentralized networks for transactions, smart contracts, and cryptocurrency management. Mobile wallets like MetaMask and Coinbase allow users to store and trade digital assets directly from their smartphones. Blockchain integration enhances security, transparency, and user control in mobile ecosystems. Challenges include energy consumption, scalability, and user education about blockchain technologies. Mobile devices make blockchain more accessible, supporting innovative applications in finance, healthcare, and supply chain management.

48. What are mobile thin clients, and where are they used?
Answer: Mobile thin clients are lightweight devices or applications that rely on remote servers for processing and storage, with the mobile device serving primarily as an interface. They are used in enterprises to provide secure access to virtual desktops and cloud-based applications. Thin clients reduce hardware costs, simplify IT management, and minimize data exposure on local devices. Challenges include ensuring network reliability and addressing latency issues. Mobile thin clients are ideal for businesses seeking secure, scalable solutions for employees who require access to centralized resources on the go.

49. How does mobile computing improve disaster recovery planning?
Answer: Mobile computing improves disaster recovery planning by providing remote access to critical systems, enabling communication during crises, and supporting data backups through cloud services. Mobile apps help organizations monitor disaster events, coordinate teams, and deploy resources effectively. Push notifications keep employees informed about safety protocols and recovery actions. Challenges include ensuring connectivity during disasters and securing sensitive information. Mobile computing enhances organizational resilience, allowing faster recovery and minimizing downtime in emergencies.

50. What is mobile contextual advertising, and how does it benefit marketers?
Answer: Mobile contextual advertising delivers ads based on a user's current activity, location, or app usage to ensure relevance and higher engagement rates. For example, a food delivery ad may appear when a user searches for restaurants nearby. Benefits include increased click-through rates, personalized user experiences, and improved return on investment for marketers. Challenges involve balancing personalization with privacy concerns and avoiding

intrusive ad practices. When implemented ethically, mobile contextual advertising strengthens brand-consumer relationships and drives conversions effectively in mobile-driven marketplaces.

51. How does mobile computing support smart energy management?
Answer: Mobile computing supports smart energy management by enabling users and utility providers to monitor, control, and optimize energy consumption through mobile apps. Consumers can adjust thermostat settings, switch appliances on or off remotely, and track real-time energy usage from their smartphones. Utility companies use mobile systems for demand forecasting, outage management, and dynamic pricing strategies. Integration with IoT devices like smart meters enhances efficiency and supports renewable energy sources. Challenges include ensuring data security, network reliability, and device compatibility. Mobile computing empowers individuals and businesses to adopt sustainable practices, reduce costs, and contribute to environmental conservation.

52. What is mobile on-demand computing, and how is it applied?
Answer: Mobile on-demand computing provides users with immediate access to computing resources, services, and applications as needed through their mobile devices. It supports cloud-based platforms that deliver scalable resources for processing, storage, and software usage. Applications include video streaming, ride-hailing services, and e-learning platforms, where users access content or services instantly. Challenges involve managing latency, ensuring robust connectivity, and maintaining security for sensitive data. Mobile on-demand computing offers flexibility, cost-efficiency, and convenience, making it a cornerstone of modern digital lifestyles and enabling businesses to scale services dynamically to meet customer demands.

53. Explain mobile biometric payment systems and their advantages.
Answer: Mobile biometric payment systems use fingerprint scans, facial recognition, or voice authentication to authorize financial transactions securely on smartphones. These systems replace traditional passwords and PINs, offering faster and more user-friendly payment experiences. Advantages include enhanced security against fraud, improved convenience, and reduced risk of credential theft. Biometric solutions are integrated into mobile wallets and payment apps, supporting contactless transactions in physical stores and online purchases. Challenges include ensuring biometric data protection, handling sensor inaccuracies, and addressing user privacy concerns. Mobile biometric payments are revolutionizing digital finance by combining security and seamless user experiences.

54. How does mobile computing enhance environmental monitoring systems?
Answer: Mobile computing enhances environmental monitoring systems by enabling real-time data collection and visualization through smartphones and IoT-connected sensors. Mobile apps track air quality, water levels, noise pollution, and waste management activities, providing actionable insights to citizens and authorities. These systems support early warnings for natural disasters like floods and forest fires. Challenges include maintaining sensor accuracy, network coverage in remote areas, and protecting environmental data privacy. Mobile computing empowers communities and governments to make informed decisions, improving environmental sustainability and promoting proactive measures to mitigate ecological challenges.

55. What is mobile network slicing in 5G, and how does it work?
Answer: Mobile network slicing in 5G divides a physical network into multiple virtual networks, each optimized for specific applications or user requirements. For example, one slice can support autonomous vehicles requiring ultra-low latency, while another handles video streaming with high bandwidth. Network slicing enables efficient resource utilization, better quality of service, and customized experiences for users. Challenges include ensuring seamless orchestration of slices, managing security across partitions, and integrating with legacy networks. Mobile network slicing is critical in 5G ecosystems, providing flexibility and supporting diverse mobile computing applications across industries like healthcare, IoT, and entertainment.

56. How does mobile computing support wearable health devices?
Answer: Mobile computing powers wearable health devices like fitness bands and smartwatches by enabling real-time data processing, synchronization, and analytics. These devices monitor metrics such as heart rate, steps, sleep patterns, and oxygen levels, sending data to mobile apps for visualization and alerts. Mobile computing enhances healthcare by supporting remote patient monitoring, personalized wellness plans, and early detection of health issues. Challenges include ensuring data accuracy, maintaining battery life, and securing sensitive health information. Wearable health

devices integrated with mobile computing improve preventive care, empower users to track wellness goals, and support medical professionals with continuous patient insights.

57. What are mobile edge applications, and why are they important?
Answer: Mobile edge applications run on computing resources located closer to the user at the network edge, reducing latency and improving performance. These apps are essential for use cases requiring real-time responsiveness, such as augmented reality (AR), autonomous vehicles, and video conferencing. By processing data locally, edge applications also enhance privacy and reduce network congestion. Challenges include deploying edge infrastructure, managing distributed data, and ensuring app scalability across diverse environments. Mobile edge applications are crucial in next-generation mobile computing, supporting seamless user experiences and enabling innovations that depend on instant processing and minimal delays.

58. Explain mobile blockchain wallets and their security features.
Answer: Mobile blockchain wallets allow users to securely store, send, and receive cryptocurrencies using their smartphones. These wallets utilize encryption, private keys, and biometric authentication to safeguard assets and prevent unauthorized access. Features like cold storage options and seed phrase backups further enhance security. Mobile blockchain wallets support decentralized finance (DeFi), enabling users to access blockchain networks for transactions and smart contracts. Challenges include educating users about safe practices and preventing phishing attacks targeting wallet credentials. Secure mobile wallets are critical for making blockchain technologies accessible and practical for mainstream adoption in digital finance ecosystems.

59. How does mobile computing support logistics and supply chain management?
Answer: Mobile computing supports logistics and supply chain management by enabling real-time tracking of shipments, inventory monitoring, and efficient route optimization. Mobile apps allow warehouse staff to scan barcodes, update records instantly, and communicate with drivers on the move. GPS integration provides visibility of delivery vehicles, ensuring timely operations and reducing delays. Challenges include network reliability in remote areas and ensuring cybersecurity for sensitive data. Mobile computing improves transparency, reduces operational costs, and enhances decision-making, making supply chains more agile and responsive to market demands.

60. What is mobile augmented commerce, and how does it transform shopping?
Answer: Mobile augmented commerce integrates augmented reality (AR) into mobile shopping experiences, allowing users to visualize products in their environment before purchasing. For example, furniture retailers use AR apps to let customers see how items fit in their homes, while fashion brands offer virtual try-ons. This approach builds customer confidence, reduces return rates, and enhances engagement. Challenges include developing high-quality AR content, ensuring app performance, and managing data privacy. Mobile augmented commerce bridges physical and digital retail experiences, transforming how consumers interact with brands and driving innovation in e-commerce.

61. Explain mobile app performance monitoring and optimization.
Answer: Mobile app performance monitoring tracks metrics such as load times, crash rates, and user interactions to ensure smooth functionality and user satisfaction. Optimization techniques include minimizing network calls, compressing media files, and streamlining code for faster processing. Tools like Firebase and AppDynamics provide real-time insights for developers to address bottlenecks. Challenges involve ensuring consistent performance across diverse devices, operating systems, and network conditions. Effective performance monitoring and optimization are critical in mobile computing to retain users, enhance engagement, and ensure positive app store ratings in competitive digital markets.

62. How does mobile computing support proximity-based services?
Answer: Mobile computing supports proximity-based services using technologies like Bluetooth Low Energy (BLE), NFC, and Wi-Fi to detect nearby devices and deliver context-specific content. Applications include contactless payments, indoor navigation, and location-targeted marketing. Retailers use BLE beacons to send personalized offers when customers enter stores, while museums guide visitors with interactive exhibits. Challenges include managing user privacy, battery consumption, and avoiding unnecessary notifications. Proximity-based services enhance user experiences by delivering timely, relevant information and fostering engagement in both commercial and public environments.

63. What is mobile virtual desktop infrastructure (VDI), and how does it work?
Answer: Mobile Virtual Desktop Infrastructure (VDI) allows users to access a virtual desktop environment hosted on a centralized server from their mobile devices. VDI supports secure, remote work by delivering applications and data without storing them locally. Employees can use corporate tools securely on personal devices in BYOD scenarios. Challenges include ensuring low latency for resource-intensive applications and securing connections against cyber threats. Mobile VDI simplifies IT management, enhances security, and provides flexibility for organizations transitioning to hybrid or remote work models.

64. How does mobile computing facilitate citizen engagement in governance?
Answer: Mobile computing facilitates citizen engagement in governance by enabling users to access government services, participate in decision-making processes, and report issues through mobile apps. Platforms allow citizens to pay taxes, apply for permits, and receive real-time alerts about public services. Social media integration empowers governments to communicate effectively and gather feedback from constituents. Challenges include digital literacy gaps, ensuring equitable access, and safeguarding sensitive data. Mobile computing strengthens transparency, accountability, and collaboration between governments and citizens, fostering more responsive and inclusive governance systems.

65. Explain mobile artificial intelligence chatbots and their use cases.
Answer: Mobile artificial intelligence (AI) chatbots are virtual assistants integrated into mobile apps that use natural language processing (NLP) to interact with users conversationally. They are used for customer support, appointment scheduling, and e-commerce recommendations. Chatbots provide instant responses, handle repetitive queries, and enhance user engagement by offering 24/7 assistance. Challenges include ensuring accurate understanding of user intent, managing complex queries, and maintaining user trust in automated systems. Mobile AI chatbots streamline workflows for businesses and create personalized, efficient interactions for users across diverse industries.

66. What are mobile smart contracts, and how are they executed?
Answer: Mobile smart contracts are self-executing agreements with terms coded into blockchain networks, accessible via mobile apps. They automatically execute actions once predefined conditions are met, removing the need for intermediaries. Applications include decentralized finance, insurance claims, and supply chain transactions. Mobile computing provides users with convenient interfaces to deploy, monitor, and interact with smart contracts on the go. Challenges include blockchain scalability, ensuring secure mobile integration, and simplifying complex contract logic for non-technical users. Mobile smart contracts promote transparency, efficiency, and trust in digital transactions across industries.

67. How does mobile computing support mobile point-of-sale (mPOS) systems?
Answer: Mobile point-of-sale (mPOS) systems transform smartphones and tablets into payment terminals using card readers, NFC technology, and payment apps. mPOS enables businesses to process transactions anywhere, enhancing convenience for customers and improving operational flexibility for vendors. Applications range from small street vendors to large retail chains offering curbside payments. Challenges include ensuring transaction security, managing connectivity in remote locations, and complying with payment regulations. Mobile computing drives mPOS adoption, supporting cashless economies and enabling businesses to serve customers more efficiently in dynamic environments.

68. Explain mobile gamification and its benefits in non-gaming sectors.
Answer: Mobile gamification applies game design elements like points, badges, and leaderboards to non-gaming applications, encouraging user engagement and motivation. Sectors like education, fitness, and marketing use gamification to enhance participation and improve outcomes. For example, language-learning apps award badges for lesson completion, while fitness apps provide challenges to keep users active. Challenges include designing meaningful rewards and avoiding user fatigue. When implemented effectively, mobile gamification fosters positive behaviors, increases retention, and drives user loyalty, making mobile computing applications more interactive and impactful.

69. How does mobile computing enhance enterprise mobility solutions?
Answer: Mobile computing enhances enterprise mobility by enabling employees to access corporate resources, communicate with teams, and perform tasks securely from their mobile devices. Enterprise mobility solutions include MDM systems, mobile apps, and cloud-based services that support remote work, field operations, and on-the-go

productivity. Challenges include ensuring data security in BYOD environments, maintaining compliance, and supporting diverse devices. Mobile computing empowers organizations to operate flexibly and respond swiftly to market changes, improving employee satisfaction and business agility in competitive industries.

70. What is mobile context-aware computing, and how is it applied?
Answer: Mobile context-aware computing uses information such as location, time, device state, and user preferences to tailor services and applications dynamically. Examples include mobile assistants adjusting notifications based on user activity, or navigation apps suggesting routes depending on traffic conditions. Context-awareness enhances personalization and improves user satisfaction. Challenges involve accurately interpreting contextual data, ensuring privacy, and minimizing battery consumption. Applied effectively, mobile context-aware computing makes applications more intelligent, responsive, and aligned with user needs in diverse scenarios.

71. How does mobile computing support digital banking solutions?
Answer: Mobile computing supports digital banking solutions by allowing users to access financial services anytime and anywhere through smartphones and tablets. Mobile banking apps enable fund transfers, bill payments, account monitoring, and loan applications. Biometric authentication and encryption secure sensitive transactions, ensuring user trust. Features like real-time notifications improve transparency and prevent fraud. Challenges include addressing cybersecurity threats, ensuring app usability, and supporting diverse device platforms. Despite these issues, mobile computing has revolutionized banking by offering convenience, reducing operational costs for banks, and enhancing financial inclusion, especially in remote or underserved areas.

72. What are mobile collaborative tools, and how do they improve productivity?
Answer: Mobile collaborative tools are applications that enable team members to communicate, share files, and work together in real time via mobile devices. Examples include Slack, Microsoft Teams, and Google Workspace. These tools support chat, video calls, document editing, and project tracking, improving workflow efficiency. Mobile access ensures employees can collaborate on the go, fostering flexible and agile work environments. Challenges include maintaining data security, managing device compatibility, and avoiding information overload. Mobile collaborative tools significantly enhance productivity, streamline operations, and support hybrid work models in today's interconnected and dynamic workplaces.

73. Explain mobile predictive maintenance and its applications.
Answer: Mobile predictive maintenance uses mobile computing and IoT sensors to monitor equipment and predict potential failures before they occur. Data collected from machines is analyzed in real time and accessed via mobile apps, allowing maintenance teams to receive alerts and plan repairs proactively. Applications include manufacturing, transportation, and energy sectors, where downtime can lead to significant costs. Challenges involve managing large datasets, ensuring sensor accuracy, and integrating predictive systems with mobile platforms. Mobile predictive maintenance reduces unplanned outages, extends asset lifespan, and enhances operational efficiency across industries.

74. How does mobile computing enable cashless economies?
Answer: Mobile computing enables cashless economies by supporting digital payment platforms such as mobile wallets, QR codes, and contactless transactions. Apps like PayPal, Google Pay, and Venmo allow users to pay bills, shop online, and transfer funds securely. Mobile banking extends financial services to unbanked populations, fostering inclusion. Challenges include ensuring cybersecurity, building user trust, and addressing connectivity issues in rural areas. Mobile computing promotes convenience, reduces dependency on physical cash, and strengthens financial systems, making it a cornerstone in the global shift towards digital and cashless economies.

75. What is mobile geolocation tracking, and how is it applied?
Answer: Mobile geolocation tracking determines the real-time location of a mobile device using GPS, Wi-Fi, and cell towers. It is applied in navigation apps, delivery tracking, ride-hailing services, and emergency response systems. Businesses use geolocation to send location-specific offers or monitor field employees. Challenges include preserving user privacy, ensuring accuracy in dense urban areas, and managing battery consumption. Mobile geolocation tracking enhances convenience, safety, and operational efficiency, making it an essential feature in diverse mobile applications for personal, commercial, and governmental use.

76. Explain mobile-based learning management systems (LMS) and their advantages.
Answer: Mobile-based learning management systems (LMS) provide educational content, assessments, and collaboration tools accessible via smartphones and tablets. They support features like microlearning, gamification, and push notifications to keep learners engaged. Advantages include flexibility for learners to study anytime and anywhere, increased interactivity, and accessibility for remote or underserved areas. Examples include Moodle, Blackboard, and Google Classroom mobile apps. Challenges include ensuring content compatibility across devices, maintaining learner focus, and protecting student data. Mobile LMS solutions revolutionize education by empowering continuous learning and promoting personalized learning paths for diverse users.

77. How does mobile computing support vehicle fleet management?
Answer: Mobile computing supports vehicle fleet management by enabling real-time tracking, route optimization, and maintenance scheduling through mobile applications. Fleet managers can monitor driver behavior, fuel consumption, and delivery statuses from their smartphones or tablets. Mobile apps provide alerts for maintenance needs and facilitate communication between drivers and operations teams. Challenges include ensuring accurate GPS tracking, data security, and integration with legacy systems. Mobile computing improves efficiency, reduces operational costs, and enhances safety in logistics and transportation industries, making it an essential tool for modern fleet operations.

78. What is mobile biometric authentication, and how does it work?
Answer: Mobile biometric authentication verifies user identity using unique biological traits such as fingerprints, facial recognition, or voice patterns. Smartphones equipped with biometric sensors capture and analyze these traits to grant secure access to devices, apps, and financial transactions. It eliminates the need for traditional passwords, enhancing security and user convenience. Challenges include preventing spoofing attacks, ensuring sensor reliability, and protecting stored biometric data. Despite these issues, mobile biometric authentication has become a standard security feature, offering fast, secure, and user-friendly authentication in mobile computing environments.

79. Explain mobile content delivery networks (CDNs) and their benefits.
Answer: Mobile content delivery networks (CDNs) distribute web content across multiple servers globally to deliver data faster to users based on their geographic location. CDNs improve mobile app and website performance by reducing latency, speeding up load times, and handling traffic spikes effectively. They are crucial for streaming services, e-commerce platforms, and global mobile applications. Benefits include enhanced user experiences, reduced bandwidth costs, and improved security against Distributed Denial of Service (DDoS) attacks. Challenges involve CDN deployment costs and maintaining content freshness. Mobile CDNs ensure reliable and efficient content delivery, supporting seamless mobile computing experiences.

80. How does mobile computing enhance workplace safety systems?
Answer: Mobile computing enhances workplace safety by enabling real-time monitoring, incident reporting, and hazard identification through mobile apps and IoT devices. Employees can report unsafe conditions instantly, receive alerts about potential risks, and access safety guidelines on their smartphones. Mobile wearables monitor worker health metrics and detect falls or exposure to hazardous environments. Challenges include ensuring network availability in remote areas and securing sensitive data. Mobile computing empowers organizations to proactively manage safety, comply with regulations, and create healthier, safer work environments across industries like construction, manufacturing, and mining.

81. What is mobile data encryption, and why is it critical?
Answer: Mobile data encryption secures sensitive information on mobile devices by converting it into unreadable code accessible only with authorized decryption keys. It protects data stored locally and during transmission over networks, safeguarding against unauthorized access and cyberattacks. Encryption is critical for financial apps, healthcare systems, and enterprise mobile devices handling confidential information. Challenges include managing encryption keys and ensuring performance on resource-limited devices. Mobile data encryption is a fundamental security measure that enhances user trust, complies with data protection laws, and supports secure mobile computing in both personal and professional contexts.

82. Explain mobile-based augmented field services and their advantages.
Answer: Mobile-based augmented field services use smartphones and tablets equipped with AR to assist technicians during on-site repairs and maintenance. AR overlays provide step-by-step instructions, visualizations of internal

components, and remote expert support through mobile devices. Advantages include faster problem resolution, reduced training times, and improved accuracy in complex tasks. Challenges involve ensuring app performance in remote areas, device compatibility, and securing sensitive operational data. Mobile-based augmented field services enhance productivity, reduce costs, and improve service quality in industries like utilities, manufacturing, and telecommunications.

83. How does mobile computing support digital supply chains?
Answer: Mobile computing supports digital supply chains by enabling real-time visibility, collaboration, and data sharing across supply chain networks through mobile devices. Warehouse staff use mobile apps for inventory management, while managers track shipments and monitor supplier performance on the go. Integration with IoT devices and cloud systems enhances automation and analytics capabilities. Challenges include data security, integrating mobile solutions with legacy systems, and ensuring reliable connectivity in remote areas. Mobile computing increases agility, reduces operational bottlenecks, and helps organizations build resilient, responsive supply chains in dynamic global markets.

84. What is mobile geofencing, and how is it applied in marketing?
Answer: Mobile geofencing creates virtual perimeters around specific geographic areas using GPS or RFID. When users enter or exit these zones, businesses send targeted notifications, offers, or advertisements to their smartphones. Retailers use geofencing to attract nearby customers with personalized discounts, while event organizers engage attendees with real-time updates. Challenges include managing battery consumption from location tracking and addressing user privacy concerns. Mobile geofencing is a powerful marketing tool that enhances customer engagement, improves conversion rates, and strengthens brand-customer relationships through location-aware strategies.

85. Explain mobile VPNs and their importance for secure connectivity.
Answer: Mobile Virtual Private Networks (VPNs) create encrypted tunnels for mobile devices to connect securely to public or corporate networks. They protect sensitive data from eavesdropping, especially on unsecured Wi-Fi networks, and enable remote employees to access company resources safely. Mobile VPNs are critical in BYOD environments and for users traveling internationally. Challenges include managing VPN performance, user authentication, and balancing security with convenience. Mobile VPNs are essential for secure mobile computing, ensuring data privacy and compliance with organizational and regulatory security standards.

86. How does mobile computing enable real-time public transportation systems?
Answer: Mobile computing enables real-time public transportation systems by integrating GPS tracking, mobile apps, and cloud platforms to provide live updates on bus and train locations, schedules, and delays. Commuters use apps to plan routes, purchase tickets, and receive alerts about service disruptions. Transport authorities use mobile data to optimize routes and improve fleet management. Challenges include ensuring accurate tracking in dense urban areas and managing network congestion during peak hours. Mobile computing improves the reliability, efficiency, and user experience of public transit systems, making urban mobility more convenient and accessible.

87. What are mobile deep learning applications, and where are they used?
Answer: Mobile deep learning applications deploy AI models on smartphones and tablets to perform complex tasks like image recognition, natural language processing, and real-time translation without relying entirely on cloud servers. Use cases include camera enhancements, virtual assistants, health monitoring, and predictive text. Advantages include lower latency, improved privacy, and offline functionality. Challenges involve optimizing deep learning models for limited device resources and ensuring battery efficiency. Mobile deep learning empowers developers to create smarter, more responsive apps that deliver advanced features directly on users' devices.

88. Explain mobile edge caching and its role in improving content delivery.
Answer: Mobile edge caching stores frequently accessed content closer to users at network edge locations, reducing the need to fetch data from distant servers. This improves load times, reduces network congestion, and enhances user experiences for mobile apps and streaming services. Edge caching is especially valuable for bandwidth-intensive content like videos and gaming. Challenges include cache management, ensuring content freshness, and handling dynamic user requests. Mobile edge caching optimizes mobile computing performance, making it critical for delivering seamless, high-speed experiences in today's data-driven applications.

89. How does mobile computing support e-voting systems?
Answer: Mobile computing supports e-voting systems by enabling secure, convenient access to voting platforms through smartphones and tablets. Voters can authenticate their identity, cast ballots, and receive confirmations from any location. Security features like encryption and biometric verification protect against fraud and unauthorized access. Challenges include ensuring system integrity, preventing cyberattacks, and addressing digital literacy gaps. Mobile e-voting increases accessibility for remote populations and supports higher voter turnout, fostering more inclusive and efficient democratic processes.

90. What is mobile machine-to-machine (M2M) communication, and how is it applied?
Answer: Mobile machine-to-machine (M2M) communication enables devices to exchange data automatically without human intervention using mobile networks. Applications include smart meters transmitting energy usage, connected vehicles sharing traffic data, and healthcare devices reporting patient vitals. Challenges involve managing large-scale device deployments, ensuring secure data transmission, and maintaining low latency. Mobile M2M communication forms the backbone of IoT ecosystems, driving automation and innovation across industries such as utilities, transportation, and healthcare.

91. How does mobile computing enhance telemedicine services?
Answer: Mobile computing enhances telemedicine services by enabling patients and healthcare providers to communicate in real time through smartphones and tablets. Video consultations, mobile diagnostic tools, and health monitoring apps allow doctors to provide care remotely, improving access for patients in rural and underserved areas. Mobile apps also help patients schedule appointments, access medical records, and receive medication reminders. Challenges include ensuring secure data transmission, maintaining regulatory compliance, and overcoming connectivity issues in remote regions. Despite these hurdles, mobile computing plays a vital role in improving healthcare delivery, reducing costs, and supporting proactive patient management.

92. What is mobile crowd sensing, and how is it used?
Answer: Mobile crowd sensing leverages data collected from mobile device sensors and user input to analyze and monitor environments or social trends. Applications include traffic monitoring, environmental mapping, and disaster response. For example, navigation apps like Waze rely on crowd-sourced data to update traffic conditions in real time. Challenges involve ensuring data quality, protecting user privacy, and incentivizing participation. Mobile crowd sensing empowers governments, researchers, and businesses to gather large-scale, real-time insights, enabling smarter decisions and fostering innovation in urban planning, public safety, and environmental sustainability.

93. Explain mobile payment gateways and their role in digital transactions.
Answer: Mobile payment gateways are platforms that process digital transactions securely between users and merchants on mobile devices. They encrypt sensitive payment data, verify credentials, and ensure seamless fund transfers. Examples include PayPal, Razorpay, and Stripe. Payment gateways support various methods such as credit cards, mobile wallets, and UPI systems, making them integral to e-commerce and in-app purchases. Challenges include ensuring robust security, preventing transaction failures, and complying with financial regulations. Mobile payment gateways simplify transactions, improve user experiences, and drive the growth of mobile commerce in today's cashless economy.

94. How does mobile computing support disaster preparedness and response?
Answer: Mobile computing supports disaster preparedness and response by enabling real-time communication, resource coordination, and situational awareness through mobile apps and devices. Emergency alerts, GPS tracking, and crowd-sourced data help authorities monitor affected areas and guide evacuation efforts. Citizens use mobile apps to report incidents, receive safety instructions, and request assistance. Challenges include ensuring network availability in disaster zones and securing sensitive data. Mobile computing enhances resilience, enabling faster, data-driven responses and improving collaboration among agencies during emergencies, ultimately saving lives and minimizing damage.

95. What is mobile social commerce, and how does it impact shopping behavior?
Answer: Mobile social commerce integrates social media platforms with e-commerce, allowing users to discover, share, and purchase products directly through mobile apps like Instagram and Facebook. Features such as shoppable posts, influencer marketing, and user-generated reviews drive engagement and purchasing decisions. Mobile devices

enable seamless browsing and transactions, encouraging impulse buys and peer-driven shopping. Challenges include balancing personalization with user privacy and ensuring secure payment processing. Mobile social commerce transforms traditional shopping experiences by combining social interaction and convenience, fostering community-based consumer behavior and expanding opportunities for businesses to reach target audiences effectively.

96. Explain mobile over-the-air (OTA) updates and their advantages.
Answer: Mobile over-the-air (OTA) updates allow device manufacturers and app developers to deploy software upgrades, security patches, and bug fixes wirelessly without requiring physical connections. Users receive notifications and can download updates directly on their mobile devices, ensuring convenience and accessibility. Advantages include faster rollout of improvements, enhanced security, and reduced dependency on service centers. Challenges involve ensuring stable connectivity during updates, managing device compatibility, and addressing potential failures mid-update. OTA updates are critical in mobile computing for maintaining device performance, safeguarding against vulnerabilities, and delivering new features efficiently.

97. How does mobile computing support real-time inventory management?
Answer: Mobile computing supports real-time inventory management by enabling employees to monitor stock levels, process orders, and update records using mobile devices. Barcode scanners, RFID readers, and inventory apps provide instant data access and improve accuracy in warehouses and retail stores. Cloud-based systems synchronize information across locations, allowing managers to make informed decisions quickly. Challenges include ensuring reliable connectivity, securing data against unauthorized access, and integrating mobile solutions with existing enterprise resource planning systems. Mobile computing streamlines operations, reduces errors, and enhances supply chain efficiency for businesses of all sizes.

98. What is mobile-based blockchain voting, and how does it work?
Answer: Mobile-based blockchain voting uses decentralized ledger technology to enable secure and transparent voting via smartphones. Blockchain ensures that each vote is encrypted, verifiable, and immutable, preventing tampering or double voting. Voters authenticate their identity using biometrics or digital IDs before casting their ballots through a mobile app. Challenges include ensuring user privacy, addressing technical literacy gaps, and building trust in the system. Mobile blockchain voting offers scalability, reduces logistical costs, and increases voter participation, particularly for citizens unable to reach physical polling stations, making it a promising solution for modernizing electoral processes.

99. Explain mobile-based augmented manufacturing solutions.
Answer: Mobile-based augmented manufacturing solutions integrate mobile devices with AR technology to assist workers in complex manufacturing tasks. Using smartphones or AR headsets, employees can access visual instructions, overlay digital models onto physical components, and receive real-time remote support from experts. These solutions enhance training, reduce errors, and improve production efficiency. Challenges include ensuring app performance in industrial environments, managing data security, and training workers to adopt new technologies. Mobile-based augmented manufacturing bridges the gap between human skills and advanced machinery, driving innovation in Industry 4.0.

100. How does mobile computing facilitate remote scientific research?
Answer: Mobile computing facilitates remote scientific research by enabling data collection, collaboration, and analysis from field locations using mobile devices. Researchers use smartphones and tablets to capture images, record observations, and transmit data to centralized databases in real time. Mobile apps support GPS tagging, cloud synchronization, and offline access for remote areas with limited connectivity. Challenges include ensuring data accuracy, device durability in harsh environments, and securing sensitive information. Mobile computing expands research capabilities, reduces logistical constraints, and fosters global scientific collaboration across disciplines.

101. What is mobile artificial intelligence (AI) personalization, and how is it applied?
Answer: Mobile artificial intelligence (AI) personalization tailors app experiences based on user behavior, preferences, and context. AI analyzes data from interactions, location, and usage patterns to deliver personalized content, recommendations, and notifications. Applications include music streaming services suggesting playlists, shopping apps offering targeted deals, and fitness apps customizing workout plans. Challenges involve maintaining user privacy, avoiding over-personalization, and ensuring algorithm transparency. Mobile AI personalization enhances

user satisfaction, increases engagement, and drives loyalty by making apps more relevant and intuitive for individual users.

102. How does mobile computing enable precision agriculture?
Answer: Mobile computing enables precision agriculture by providing farmers with tools to monitor soil conditions, weather patterns, and crop health through mobile devices. Sensors and drones transmit real-time data to mobile apps, supporting data-driven decisions for irrigation, fertilization, and pest management. Farmers receive alerts and recommendations tailored to specific field zones, improving efficiency and yields. Challenges include ensuring network connectivity in rural areas, addressing cost barriers, and providing digital literacy training. Mobile computing empowers sustainable farming practices, reduces resource wastage, and enhances food security globally.

103. Explain mobile cloud gaming and its advantages.
Answer: Mobile cloud gaming allows users to play high-performance video games on smartphones by streaming them from remote servers, eliminating the need for powerful hardware. Services like NVIDIA GeForce NOW and Xbox Cloud Gaming provide access to large game libraries on demand. Advantages include reduced device storage requirements, cross-platform access, and the ability to play advanced games on budget smartphones. Challenges involve managing latency, ensuring stable internet connectivity, and reducing data consumption. Mobile cloud gaming democratizes access to premium gaming experiences, transforming mobile devices into versatile entertainment hubs.

104. What is mobile-based e-learning gamification, and why is it effective?
Answer: Mobile-based e-learning gamification integrates game mechanics such as rewards, challenges, and leaderboards into educational apps to motivate learners. Features like badges for achievements, timed quizzes, and interactive storytelling make learning engaging and enjoyable. Gamification is effective because it fosters competition, increases retention, and encourages consistent participation. Examples include Duolingo and Khan Academy mobile apps. Challenges involve designing meaningful rewards and ensuring that gamification aligns with learning objectives. Mobile gamification enhances knowledge acquisition, making education accessible and interactive for users of all ages.

105. How does mobile computing support urban mobility solutions?
Answer: Mobile computing supports urban mobility solutions by enabling real-time navigation, ride-sharing apps, and integrated ticketing systems for public transport. Users rely on mobile apps to plan multi-modal journeys, track vehicle locations, and pay fares conveniently. Transport authorities use mobile data analytics to optimize routes and manage traffic flow. Challenges include ensuring equitable access to mobile solutions and managing data privacy. Mobile computing improves efficiency, reduces congestion, and enhances the commuter experience, contributing to the development of smart, sustainable urban transportation systems.

106. What is mobile peer-to-peer lending, and how does it work?
Answer: Mobile peer-to-peer (P2P) lending platforms connect borrowers and lenders directly through mobile apps, bypassing traditional financial institutions. Users register, verify identities, and negotiate loan terms within the platform, which facilitates secure transactions. Algorithms assess borrower credibility using alternative data such as mobile usage patterns and social media activity. Challenges include managing default risks, ensuring regulatory compliance, and safeguarding sensitive financial data. Mobile P2P lending promotes financial inclusion, offering flexible credit options to underserved populations and enabling investors to diversify their portfolios.

107. Explain mobile multi-cloud strategies and their importance.
Answer: Mobile multi-cloud strategies involve using multiple cloud providers to host mobile app services, ensuring better performance, scalability, and resilience. By distributing workloads across providers like AWS, Azure, and Google Cloud, businesses avoid vendor lock-in and mitigate risks from service outages. Mobile apps benefit from faster content delivery and improved reliability for global users. Challenges include managing interoperability, ensuring consistent security policies, and monitoring costs across platforms. Multi-cloud strategies are crucial for mobile computing, enabling developers to build robust applications that meet user demands efficiently and securely.

108. How does mobile computing enhance personalized marketing campaigns?
Answer: Mobile computing enhances personalized marketing campaigns by leveraging user data from apps, browsing

history, and location services to deliver targeted advertisements and offers. Marketers use mobile analytics to segment audiences and customize messaging based on user behavior and preferences. Push notifications and in-app promotions increase engagement and conversion rates. Challenges include respecting privacy regulations, avoiding over-targeting, and ensuring data security. Mobile computing enables businesses to connect with customers meaningfully, fostering loyalty and improving the effectiveness of digital marketing efforts.

109. What is mobile-based peer-to-peer file sharing, and how does it work?
Answer: Mobile-based peer-to-peer (P2P) file sharing allows users to transfer data directly between devices without relying on centralized servers. Technologies like Wi-Fi Direct, Bluetooth, and NFC facilitate fast sharing of photos, videos, and documents. Applications include SHAREit and AirDrop, which provide user-friendly interfaces for seamless transfers. Challenges involve ensuring secure transfers, managing compatibility across devices, and preventing unauthorized access. Mobile P2P file sharing enhances convenience, particularly in offline environments, and supports collaborative workflows in both personal and professional settings.

110. Explain mobile knowledge management systems and their applications.
Answer: Mobile knowledge management systems (KMS) provide access to organizational knowledge bases, training materials, and collaborative tools on smartphones and tablets. Employees use mobile KMS apps to search documentation, share insights, and solve problems on the go. Applications include customer support teams accessing product FAQs and field workers retrieving technical manuals. Challenges involve securing sensitive information, ensuring offline functionality, and promoting user adoption. Mobile KMS enhances productivity, facilitates knowledge sharing, and supports informed decision-making, making it essential for modern enterprises in dynamic, mobile-centric environments.

111. How does mobile computing support predictive analytics in businesses?
Answer: Mobile computing supports predictive analytics by enabling businesses to analyze user behavior, market trends, and operational data in real time via mobile applications. Smartphones collect valuable data on customer preferences and engagement, which AI algorithms process to forecast demand and personalize services. For instance, e-commerce apps use predictive analytics to recommend products, while logistics companies optimize delivery routes. Challenges include ensuring data privacy, managing computational limitations of mobile devices, and integrating analytics tools across platforms. Mobile computing empowers organizations to make proactive, data-driven decisions, enhancing customer satisfaction and operational efficiency in competitive markets.

112. What is mobile-based real-time language translation, and how does it work?
Answer: Mobile-based real-time language translation uses AI-powered applications on smartphones to convert spoken or written content into another language instantly. Apps like Google Translate use camera input to translate signs and documents or voice recognition for conversations. This functionality is enabled by cloud computing and on-device processing, allowing users to communicate across language barriers effectively. Challenges include ensuring translation accuracy, managing resource constraints on devices, and supporting less common languages. Mobile translation tools are invaluable for travelers, businesses, and multicultural collaborations, making global communication more accessible and seamless.

113. Explain mobile serverless computing and its advantages.
Answer: Mobile serverless computing allows developers to build and deploy mobile app functionalities without managing server infrastructure. Cloud providers handle the backend operations, automatically scaling resources based on demand. Advantages include reduced development costs, faster deployment, and simplified maintenance. Mobile apps benefit from serverless architectures by achieving greater flexibility and responsiveness during traffic spikes. Challenges involve debugging distributed systems, managing cold start delays, and ensuring security. Serverless computing empowers mobile developers to focus on user experience and innovation rather than infrastructure management, accelerating time-to-market for modern mobile applications.

114. How does mobile computing support the gig economy?
Answer: Mobile computing supports the gig economy by providing platforms that connect freelancers and service providers to clients through mobile apps. Applications like Uber, Fiverr, and TaskRabbit enable workers to find jobs, communicate with clients, and receive payments directly from their smartphones. Mobile technologies facilitate real-time task allocation, GPS tracking, and secure financial transactions. Challenges include ensuring fair labor practices,

protecting worker data, and managing regulatory compliance across regions. Mobile computing empowers flexibility and autonomy for gig workers while offering businesses scalable solutions to meet dynamic workforce needs in diverse industries.

115. What is mobile IoT device orchestration, and why is it important?
Answer: Mobile IoT device orchestration involves managing and coordinating the interactions of multiple IoT devices through mobile applications. It allows users to control smart home ecosystems, industrial machinery, or healthcare devices from a single interface on their smartphone. Orchestration ensures devices communicate effectively, automates workflows, and resolves conflicts between interconnected systems. Challenges include ensuring interoperability across brands, maintaining security, and optimizing network bandwidth. Mobile IoT orchestration simplifies complex environments, providing users with seamless control and enabling efficient operations in both personal and professional IoT applications.

116. Explain mobile digital twins in industrial operations.
Answer: Mobile digital twins replicate physical assets or processes in virtual models that can be monitored and analyzed through mobile devices. In industrial operations, they allow engineers to visualize equipment performance, simulate scenarios, and detect potential failures remotely. Mobile access to digital twins enables on-the-go monitoring and faster decision-making in industries like manufacturing, energy, and logistics. Challenges involve synchronizing real-time data, protecting intellectual property, and managing computational requirements for detailed simulations. Mobile digital twins enhance efficiency, reduce downtime, and support predictive maintenance in complex industrial ecosystems.

117. How does mobile computing support secure healthcare data sharing?
Answer: Mobile computing supports secure healthcare data sharing by enabling encrypted communication between patients, healthcare providers, and medical systems through mobile apps. Features like biometric authentication and blockchain integration protect sensitive records during transmission and storage. Mobile health platforms allow patients to share lab results, prescriptions, and vitals with their doctors in real time, improving treatment coordination. Challenges include compliance with regulations like HIPAA, ensuring interoperability between systems, and safeguarding against cyberattacks. Secure mobile data sharing enhances patient care, reduces administrative burdens, and fosters collaboration across healthcare networks.

118. What is mobile-based smart grid management, and how does it work?
Answer: Mobile-based smart grid management uses smartphones and tablets to monitor and control energy grids in real time. Utility companies leverage mobile apps to track energy consumption, detect faults, and respond to outages swiftly. Consumers use mobile interfaces to manage smart meters, adjust energy usage, and receive notifications about power fluctuations. Challenges include securing critical infrastructure against cyber threats, ensuring consistent connectivity, and integrating legacy systems with mobile technologies. Mobile computing enhances grid reliability, supports renewable energy integration, and empowers users to participate actively in energy conservation initiatives.

119. Explain mobile blockchain-enabled supply chain tracking.
Answer: Mobile blockchain-enabled supply chain tracking provides transparency and traceability by recording every step of a product's journey on a decentralized ledger accessible via mobile devices. Users can scan QR codes to verify product authenticity, origin, and handling conditions. Businesses monitor supplier compliance, reduce fraud, and enhance trust with stakeholders. Challenges include ensuring blockchain scalability, integrating with existing supply chain systems, and training users to adopt the technology. Mobile blockchain solutions revolutionize logistics by delivering real-time insights and fostering accountability throughout the supply chain network.

120. How does mobile computing support hybrid work environments?
Answer: Mobile computing supports hybrid work environments by providing employees with access to corporate applications, collaboration tools, and secure data storage from any location. Mobile apps facilitate communication through video conferencing, instant messaging, and project management platforms like Asana and Trello. Features like mobile VPNs ensure secure access to sensitive files while working remotely. Challenges include balancing security with user convenience, managing device compatibility, and addressing potential distractions in mobile workflows. Mobile computing empowers businesses to maintain productivity and flexibility, enabling seamless transitions between office-based and remote work arrangements.

121. What is mobile fog computing, and how does it differ from cloud computing?
Answer: Mobile fog computing extends cloud capabilities by processing data closer to the device, at the network edge, rather than relying solely on centralized servers. This reduces latency, conserves bandwidth, and supports real-time mobile applications like autonomous vehicles and augmented reality. Fog computing differs from cloud computing by decentralizing data processing to improve speed and responsiveness. Challenges include managing distributed resources, ensuring security, and orchestrating complex networks. Mobile fog computing bridges the gap between devices and cloud infrastructure, enabling intelligent, responsive mobile services in latency-sensitive use cases.

122. Explain mobile digital wallets and their role in financial inclusion.
Answer: Mobile digital wallets store payment information securely on smartphones, enabling users to make cashless transactions conveniently. Examples include Apple Pay, Paytm, and M-Pesa. Digital wallets are pivotal in promoting financial inclusion by providing banking services to unbanked populations in remote regions. Users can pay bills, transfer funds, and access microloans without physical bank branches. Challenges involve ensuring transaction security, building user trust, and maintaining compliance with financial regulations. Mobile wallets empower individuals and businesses, fostering economic participation and supporting cashless ecosystems globally.

123. How does mobile computing support renewable energy systems?
Answer: Mobile computing supports renewable energy systems by enabling real-time monitoring, control, and optimization of solar panels, wind turbines, and energy storage devices through mobile applications. Users track energy production, consumption, and storage levels on their smartphones. Utility providers use mobile data to forecast energy demand and balance grids effectively. Challenges include integrating mobile apps with diverse hardware and ensuring cybersecurity for critical systems. Mobile computing promotes sustainability by giving users and energy providers tools to manage and scale renewable energy solutions efficiently.

124. What is mobile-based immersive learning, and how is it applied?
Answer: Mobile-based immersive learning uses augmented reality (AR) and virtual reality (VR) on smartphones to create interactive, experiential educational environments. Students explore 3D models, participate in virtual labs, and engage with simulations through mobile apps. Applications range from medical training to STEM education and workforce development. Challenges include device performance limitations, developing high-quality content, and ensuring accessibility for all learners. Mobile immersive learning enhances engagement, supports personalized education, and prepares users for real-world scenarios in innovative, cost-effective ways.

125. Explain mobile digital signatures and their importance in secure communication.
Answer: Mobile digital signatures use cryptographic techniques to authenticate the sender and ensure the integrity of documents or messages transmitted via smartphones. They verify the identity of users and confirm that data has not been altered during transmission. Mobile digital signatures are used in financial transactions, legal agreements, and e-governance services. Challenges include managing encryption keys, ensuring compatibility across devices, and complying with digital signature regulations. Mobile digital signatures enhance trust, streamline workflows, and support secure, paperless communication in mobile computing ecosystems.

Printed at Repro India Ltd.